Slow Schooling

A Return to Learning as an
Enjoyable Lifestyle

Slow Schooling

A Return to Learning as an
Enjoyable Lifestyle

KERI MAE LAMAR

A Happy Home Media
KINGSTON, WASHINGTON

Copyright © 2023 by Keri Mae Lamar.

All rights reserved. No part of this publication may be reproduced, distributed or transmitted in any form or by any means, including photocopying, recording, or other electronic or mechanical methods, without the prior written permission of the publisher, except in the case of brief quotations embodied in critical reviews and certain other noncommercial uses permitted by copyright law. For permission requests, write to the publisher, addressed "Attention: Permissions Coordinator", at the address below.

Keri Mae Lamar
AHappyHomeMedia.com and
AHappyHomeMedia.substack.com
P.O. Box 1304; Kingston, WA 98346

Author photograph: Logan Lamar

Links referenced or recommended in this book may be affiliate links, to which the author earns a small commission.

Blog excerpts taken from the early A Happy Home blogging of Keri Mae Lamar.

All scripture from the authorized King James Version.

Slow Schooling/Keri Mae Lamar - 1st. ed.
ISBN 978-0-9961100-4-4

10 9 8 7 6 5 4 3 2 1

To all of the parents...

who believe their children should be able to live a whole life at home and learn academics along the way as they grow up in their own time, but feel inadequate to the task of educating them given their own ordinary lives.

You who love your children best...

tell them about Jesus, give them sunshine, read them books, offer them the gifts of boredom and quietness, talk with them along the way, honor their interests, and let them know they're needed and cherished. You're not "preparing" for real life; you're living it.

Enjoy them.

Home is the best place for teaching many things, first and most important of which is how to think for one's self.

– Laura Ingalls Wilder

CONTENTS

Preface xiii

Start Here xix

1. Schooling vs. Education 1
2. The Real World 15
3. What Slow Schooling is NOT 27
4. What Slow Schooling IS 35
5. Why Not Government Schooling? 47
6. On Being "Qualified" to Teach 69
7. Equipping and Caring for the Teacher 79
8. Teaching and Training 97
9. Toddlers to Big Kids 111
10. Middles Through the Teen Years 135
11. Life Skills 145
12. Experiences 167
13. Teaching the Bible 175
14. Teaching Writing 185
15. Teaching Reading 195
16. Teaching History, Science, Math 207
17. Teaching the Fine Arts 215

18. Real Life Helps Along the Way.............227
- Scheduling
- Toddlers
- Finances
- Homemaking
- Drug-Free Health
- Media
- Toys and Play
- The Local Church
- Special Needs and Adoption
- On Finding a Mentor

Keeping It in Perspective...255

"Slow School" (The Original Blog Post).......................261
Extras...273
Endnotes, Links, & References................................291
Jottings...307

Other Books by Keri Mae..323

Preface

This book almost didn't get published.

It sounded like a good idea to write it after the success of a blog post I wrote called "Slow School". [You can read the original blog at the back of this book]. The main gist of the post was "Relax, already!" I saw and heard from too many homeschooling parents who were trying to get *everything in* while running over the relationships they had with their kids. I know that this partly stems from the feeling we parents somehow need to justify how we're raising our kids, or prove to the world that

SLOW SCHOOLING

we're not really messing things up. Well, NEWSFLASH: Every parent messes up and drives their kids nuts at some point(s), just as every kid rebels and dishonors their parents in some way(s). But at the end of their childhoods, don't you still want to have a good relationship with your kid?

Apparently, this post struck a nerve. It even attracted the attention of high profile bloggers. So I wrote the book.

And then I sat on it. So many reasons why, but if I dig down, it was mostly due to fear of man and fear of failure. Who was I to basically ask homeschooling parents to relax a little? I was a terrible model for my children in this! When I finally got brave enough to send off the manuscript to an editor, it came back with an angry response (and cancellation). How was

PREFACE

I supposed to know she was not only public schooling her kids, but an avid proponent of it? So now I was fearful of responses from both homeschoolers and public schoolers. Fear of man, check.

Then COVID hit. The lockdowns. The sometimes welcomed, sometimes forced, homeschooling. All of the sudden, parents were getting real life videos into their child's educational system, and some of it was disturbing. They were also changing their perceptions of homeschooling as it wasn't as bad as they had been led to believe.[1] As states begin allowing students to return to school, many millions of parents decided to keep homeschooling their children as they could see for themselves not only the positive impact of home education, but of insuring a safe environment.[1]

SLOW SCHOOLING

I looked at this file of a manuscript I had written. I really wanted to share with parents that it's ok if your child only spends five hours a week in academics. They're still more likely to outperform their peers in standardized tests, graduate, and succeed in college than their counterparts in formal institutional schooling.[1] It's ok to relax, slow school, and enjoy their very short childhood in the context of your loving home.

I found another editor.

So I suppose I need to give a warning of sorts. I believe homeschooling to not only be a blessing, but to be better than other educational choices in most cases. This should be obvious, because if I didn't believe that, I wouldn't be doing it. Also, I am a Christian woman who knows that the Bible is the Word of God, and

PREFACE

that all scripture is profitable, so teaching my children what it says is not only of priority, but the very reason why we can say teaching subjects such as logic, reasoning, writing, reading, math, science, art, and history are important. I make no apology for standing on the Word.

I pray you will be inspired, encouraged, and challenged. Most of all, I pray the very best for you and your children, and that you will use wisely this short time you have with them to invest diligently and lovingly into their lives. You do more good than you know just by being present with them on a daily basis through the good and bad. Grow them up, and enjoy the journey.

– KML

Start Here

It's morning. My eyes open to tentative sunshine coming through the thick textured curtains, and I stretch. Saturday. I can hear my little brother already up, banging away at drawers, doors, toys, his voice full of mmm's and rrr's as little metallic cars race over carpet folds and crash into one another.

I know how the morning will go. Dad will make Eggo waffles with Mrs. Butterworth looking regally on. He will read the newspaper in his slippers and at some point will take Tinker, our pomeranian, for a walk. Mom will

SLOW SCHOOLING

wash all of the dishes, sanitize wherever we've been, and then get busy ridding dust and dirt. My brother, Larry, will finally tire of his matchbox cars, pad into the family chatter, and ask for Fruit Loops with his waffles. And I...I will read a chapter of Archie Andrews and then race out the door. I will jump onto my pink banana seat bicycle, pump my legs, and seek out friends. They, too, are flowing from homes, blinking into the sunshine, and grabbing bikes and balls.

Roller skates rush down sidewalks, clicking over breaks between the squares. Laughter, shouting, shrieks of tag. Jump ropes, soccer, chatty girlfriends sitting on curbs and stretching legs and pulling gum.

It's Saturday morning.

START HERE

I think about this, my childhood, especially when I cruise down a suburban neighborhood full of single family homes, square checkerboard garages placed front and center. Sidewalks roll like hills in front of yards polka dotted with dandelions. But it's like a ghost town.

I see at least one blow up pool with a slide, evidence of water play. One young teen boy, walking his dog—the dog alone looks excited to be outside. What I want to know is...where are all of the children? I hear them in my mind, but my eyes relay the truth.

Where is the pick-up soccer game? The underdogs at the playground with show-off boys zipping their 10-speed bikes underneath screaming preteen girls on swings?

SLOW SCHOOLING

It's still Saturday. But it feels a bit empty is all.

The paradox is this: childhood is disappearing even as many adults today eschew the idea of growing up. Childhood, defined as that time of life between conception and puberty, are getting exposed to some experiences, knowledge, and attainments that even mature adults ought not to become aware of. Today, 60% of adults report experiencing crime, violence, abuse or other childhood trauma before they were 17 years old. Twenty-five percent were victims of robbery or a witness to a violent act, and nearly half of all children and adolescents were assaulted at least once in the past year.[1] Even children in the womb are robbed of their potential, with the epidemic of painkiller and heroin use now causing the birth of a drug-addicted baby every half an hour in

START HERE

the US.[2] Pornography is not only more prevalent and popular with the secrecy of online access, it is a global $97 billion industry[3] that children either easily stumble upon, or are purposely introduced to, at younger ages. Sexual activity in all forms is being pushed as "education" even for kindergartners.[4]

Young people, however, are content to refrain from taking on the traditional rites of passage into adulthood, from marrying to taking responsibility for children, an income, or even a house.[5] The average age of a gamer is 31 years old[6] and coloring books for adults have become more popular every year, with 12 million copies sold (and, presumably colored in), in 2015.[7] Adults are living in a post-modern world, questioning the value of work, faith, and ethics even as they live in a very real world of paying very real electric bills and grappling

SLOW SCHOOLING

with terrorism that sees no problem sending in a 13 year old to be a suicide bomber.[8]

What's this all have to do with slow schooling? Well, let me ask you a question first.. Why did you pick up this book?

Perhaps you are grieved by the trauma and sorrow today's children witness and experience.

Perhaps you are discouraged by the practices in the schools, and want other options for your own children.

Perhaps you are wanting to steer your children away from the current cultural revolution of relativism and godlessness.

Perhaps you see the changes on the horizon and want to better prepare your children for a

START HERE

future that is very much different than your own generation.

Perhaps you want more real life experiences with your children, and you'd like to participate in them alongside.

Perhaps you want to foster a close family relationship.

Perhaps you want your children to have times of lollygagging and boredom in which to cultivate imaginations.

Perhaps you desire your children to have more opportunities to serve and love their neighbors and their world at large.

Perhaps you recognize that the time you have to invest into your children's lives is woefully swift and short, and you have much to share with them.

Perhaps you are dismayed by the curriculum in the schools, or are distressed by the test scores coming out from them.

Perhaps you are concerned by the lack of respect for your familial, religious or cultural worldview, and the indoctrination of the antithesis of it.

Perhaps you are already homeschooling and are burned out.

Perhaps you feel ill-equipped to parent your child, much less teach them.

START HERE

Perhaps you are overwhelmed by the laws, choices and sheer amounts of curriculum available to parents such as yourself.

Perhaps you need a new vision for your children and your family.

If so, then perhaps I wrote this book for you. This book began as a blog post that went viral on Facebook, which is a little ironic as I am not on Facebook at all. The take-away on that Slow Schooling post was "Relax, already," and we as parents need to hear those words more. Somehow we've gotten the idea that parenting is not only difficult (and it can be!), but that home educating our own children is an impossibility, only responsibly delegated to the professionals.

SLOW SCHOOLING

And who am I? I'm a former government school educator and NEA member, paid to provide inservice to other teachers in the area of language arts and a leader in organizing research groups in multiple areas of interest. I left my first baby at home with her father to pursue the career-and-mommy-mix path, and came home for good when she was 9 months old. That daughter graduated from our homeschool to apprentice with a renowned tailor, play in an orchestra with her violin and viola, work in our family business, and further her education on her own through collegiate classes and travel. We have eight more children, two of whom were born with Down syndrome. I wrote a book on overcoming the distractions of our current age (mostly digital), titled PRESENT, and I continue to live out the dream of being fully involved in and inspired

START HERE

by the beautiful children within my happy home.

As a Christian wife and mother, I see all of my children as God's handiwork, made in His image, perfectly unique and equipped to bring their own amazing and marvelous talents and gifts into a lost and hurting world. We long to love our neighbors in truth, and we'd love to see your family thrive.

Get ready for better Saturdays.

Kingston, Washington
October 2023

1

Schooling vs. Education

BLOG

"The School Thing"

Thursday, July 17, 2008, 07:16am

Comment from a reader:

"We have homeschooled almost 18 years now...and I started out with the seat work at the table bit...but like you, I wanted more for my kiddos.... I have all boys,I wanted each of them to be godly men, wonderful husbands, and

SLOW SCHOOLING

great fathers...so we tossed 80% of the books most years.... We read lots of books...separate...as a family.... We talked about them...and we did math...maybe 2-3 times a week. The boys were able to explore their interests peppered with real life instruction. For a month they worked with a neighbor learning how to shingle a roof, followed by volunteering at Habitat and learning other skills. One saved his money from raising rabbits and went to the state surplus auction where he bid on a hundred computers, swapped out parts and built 35 good ones which he sold on eBay and made a dandy profit. He spent HOURS absorbed in that which he could not have done had I forced the book work. They took

SCHOOLING vs. EDUCTION

mission trips to Honduras, Maine & NY after Ground Zero to feed volunteers. They hiked mountains and worked in soup kitchens, learned how to run a tiller and plant a garden. They bought old cars and learned how to swap out transmissions and what a universal joint was.

"So, despite my schooling fears, I woke each morning and committed our learning to the Lord for each child. And at night my hubby and I would pray together for us to be able to guide them where HE wanted them to go.

"The results: The oldest is 27 and engaged to a very wonderful woman. He owns a landscape business that specializes in solar lighting and

SLOW SCHOOLING

is working on finishing up his degree at NCSU in Sociology and Public Service where he hopes to work for a non-profit. He is the author of the book, 'The Faces Have Names,' a pictorial on the homeless in America.

"#2 son is married to a lovely woman (he is the computer kiddo mentioned above). He works in IT from home where he and his wife hope to have a house full of children. He and his wife have a music ministry where they sing together at different events.

"#3 son volunteered at Ground Zero when he was 15 and just returned from Iraq with a Purple Heart, Bronze Star with Valor & a Medal of Commendation for his service.

SCHOOLING vs. EDUCTION

He will settle in as a police officer and continue volunteering with at-risk kids as soon as his wounds are patched up (we seriously need a good chiropractor!!!)

"#4 son will play basketball at Liberty University as soon as he graduates and wants to coach at a Christian school or college.

"It works. It works by committing it to the Lord...."

There is a tremendous amount of research and studies now that prove that homeschooling results in children who are successful, happy, and meeting their unique potentials while they

SLOW SCHOOLING

are in turn blessing their communities. [See Dr. Rudner's *The Scholastic Achievement and Demographic Characteristics of Home School Students in 1998*, for example of even the success of early homeschoolers.[1]] However, success of an endeavor does not depend upon whatever "study" comes about on whatever parameters it has set; it depends on how the individual, him or herself, defines success. For one, it will be a high GPA. For another, it will be a profitable business. And so on.

Noah Webster's *1828 American Dictionary of the English Language*, an early—and still relevant— masterpiece of the English language, defines schooling as "to teach with superiority; to tutor; to chide and admonish; to reprove." The sense here is that unlike the Latin heritage of the word (ironically, "a place where leisure is enjoyed"), schooling involves engaging

SCHOOLING vs. EDUCTION

assembled students under the direct instruction of one or more teachers for the purpose of improvement or learning. But, learning what, we may ask.

The very nature of the school system is to train people to follow the clock, to move obediently from one place to another (in straight lines), and to more or less accept whatever is taught as primary importance. Teachers feed the students the subject at hand, chosen by remote and invisible politicians and lobbyists, and students consume it. With dozens of people in one classroom, it is impossible to fully individualize instruction without bucking the system of a chosen curriculum for everyone to attain mastery in. Teachers that do so are not commended, except, perhaps, by their students. John Taylor Gatto is a well known example of this.[2]

SLOW SCHOOLING

The goal of a systemized school is to produce consumers and employees. Students are expected and rewarded to accept the teaching and do the homework, and are rewarded with vague letter grades and scholarships where they, presumably, will go on to do more of the same, eventually ending up driven as consumers using debt, obligation, and societal pressure to keep up with the herd.

Slow schooling, however, differs from institutionalized schooling. This slow schooling type of education concerns itself with the forming of habits that will enable the student to not only have the tools to become producers (not just consumers), but will have the drive and imagination to do so. Slow schooling concerns itself not only with what books to read, but with how to interact with a book, to think while reading, to place it in context

SCHOOLING vs. EDUCTION

within the world at large and to attempt to understand the author's worldview and intention. Entrepreneurs and producers are educated via slow schooling, not merely moved en masse through a broken system.

Slow schooling is about true education. It respects the child's innate interests and talents and treats him as a unique individual. It meets the child where he or she is. If he has already fully grasped the concept about electrical circuits while hanging around his uncle, does he need to read the chapter in the science book on it? If she is doing math in her head correctly while baking to double for the crowd of eaters, does she need that page of fractions to do? Well, maybe. But, maybe not.

Much of our confidence in our children's education lies in their completed worksheets,

SLOW SCHOOLING

their report cards, their graduation rates, and perhaps we've gotten a bit idolatrous of high SAT scores. Is this right? Shouldn't at least some of our confidence lie in their love for God, their ability to care for animals, or to love one another? Yes, we want them to know how to read and write (and we'll discuss why later on), but don't we also want our children to know how to tie knots, cook rice, and do laundry? How about knowing the names of plants and birds outside of their windows, having some rich poetry in memory, and a good directional sense for when the GPS breaks.

I've long wanted to speak with Daniel's mother. Yes, THAT Daniel from the book in the Bible, the one who as a teen was ripped from his family and country, deported to a foreign land, served under a pagan king and yet still remained steadfast and faithful in service and

SCHOOLING vs. EDUCTION

prayer, even in the face of death. Or to have tea with Susanna Wesley, whose children grew to write magnificent hymns and have such passion for the lost. Or to walk with the mother of Moses; how DID he come to remember his people, to turn aside in wonder at the burning bush and to hear the Lord's voice? If my children ever live in such circumstances, will they have such passion and conviction? Or am I simply satisfied with their test scores? What is the point of learning anything if it is not to grow into wise and loving people?

And yet I still feel the pressure as a homeschooler to go through a curriculum, give and mark off assignments, and follow a book. I want to know the "right way" to homeschool, the guaranteed approach that will produce very intelligent and respectable adults on fire for Jesus! However, when I ask the Lord what

SLOW SCHOOLING

that perfect approach might be, He simply says, "But seek ye first the kingdom of God, and his righteousness; and all these things shall be added unto you" (Matthew 6:33).

Our confidence cannot be in the means of gaining academic knowledge even as our nation begins burdening our students more with the expectation they will compete with other nations' children's test scores (yes, those children, who spend the majority of their waking hours in memorization drills to pass exams—those children, who even at the age of ten, are committing suicide due to the pressure).[3] Instead, our confidence must be in the One who knows every hair on our child's head. We cannot put our trust in "the best school" or in "the best reviewed curriculum" but in God, who put these children in our lives not only for us to bring up, but to bring US up. And clearly, God cares

SCHOOLING vs. EDUCTION

about those relationships we have with them. He also knows and allows every interruption, illness, and hardship into our lives, and those, too, are very educational, even when happiness and worldly success seem elusive.

BLOG
"June Gloom or June Glee?"
Wednesday, June 14, 2006, 11:22 AM

> I want them to know and love God, to know how to live with and care for others, and to know how to learn. I want them to know how to work, and to work well in their chores and other life skills. I want them to play hard, using their bodies, imaginations and creativity. I want them to read

SLOW SCHOOLING

well, and to be hungry to find out more about whatever it is they want to learn about. I want them to jump up and down wagging their tongues in glee when I open up a new box of books for them to peruse...like they do already. The degree I got for teaching woefully equipped me for this sort of juggling, and if anything, hindered me from seeing the big picture of what family life could be like. So I have been learning all kinds of things (like how to keep a home, how to cook, how to not lose my mind...) along with my children, and I'm growing and learning along with them....

2

The Real World

BLOG

"Thoughts on a Happy Home"

Sunday, February 25, 2007, 03:35pm

> I think at times there is a fear that they are going to end up uninformed about and unready for the "real world", and that they are going to miss out on "experiences" that somehow have become the holy grails of growing up....

SLOW SCHOOLING

The "real world" I gained by schooling through 12 years of almost perfect attendance in the public schools. I went on to five years at the University of California not only for a BA degree, but credentials to teach dozens of children at a time in a classroom setting. I was a "good student" with good grades, good behavior, and a love of doing homework and learning. However, once I became a "real" adult, I realized that I didn't really learn much other than how to follow the rules, do assignments given to me, and to do my best to not disappoint my elders. Three times in my recollection did I attempt pardon from ridiculous assignments that made no practical sense and failed from getting

THE REAL WORLD

freed from them. So even though I graduated university with honors, I certainly could not attain much of the "formidable lists" of goals that were presumably gained by children under the age of 12 a hundred years previous.[1]

If a child learns how to read, measure, discern worldviews, cook a meal, grow a garden, fix a tire, and treat a wound, is he ready for the real world? If she learns how to research, how to write, change a diaper, recognize flora and fauna and actually care, is she ready for the real world? I think before we throw around this notion that children who are educated in alternative ways aren't ready for the "real world," we ought to not only ask for a definition of terms, but take them in hand and have a real look around at how we truly live our lives.

Homeschoolers are not immune to the idea. In fact, there is now a whole industry built around providing workbooks and busywork to help mark the time during school time at home. Except we at home are not running a school. We are constantly in a flow of preparation-consumption. We prepare the food, we eat the food. We teach our kids to read, and then you can't keep them from reading even if you tried. We also add in explanation and teach as we go throughout the day: why this food and not that one, how we as a family relate to one another, even what makes the world go round. This kind of education is a threat to a culture of conformity.

THE REAL WORLD

It's unfair to pigeonhole individual, unique children into the same methods and speeds of learning. Homeschoolers are famous for wanting to cover as much ground as possible in as wide a swath as possible, so that their children will not only be well-equipped for whatever comes, but that they will be exonerated if questioned about things left untaught. The problem there, of course, is that it is impossible even for any school to reach such fantastical goals. Those goals, instead, narrowly focus on getting students ready for the "real world," the world in which I successfully worked a job in my younger years that would not even call me by my name, but by "Employee 99."

The truth is, there are some things children never have to learn AT ALL. It is a pleasure and profit to spend a whole week, or a month, or a year, on whatever you or they are gung-

SLOW SCHOOLING

ho about, whether it is learning bird names or studying Leif Erikson. It is sad I gave up on learning higher math and chemistry lab, even though I loved those subjects, because teachers never let me approach things in my own visual way of learning. Instead, it was "do page 54...then 55...then 56...." I don't remember much from textbook learning other than answering the questions at the end of chapters (in complete sentences of course). Do you happen to remember the English monarchy? In order? And if so, how has that been made useful to you?

Here is a list from my then 6 year old about what she wanted to learn:

- ✓ grow flowers
- ✓ sew

THE REAL WORLD

- ✓ make paper flowers
- ✓ make dolls
- ✓ make bows
- ✓ plant a sea of flowers
- ✓ make a dress
- ✓ make a basket
- ✓ make a book
- ✓ make a tin car
- ✓ do corking
- ✓ cooking

Now, if we did nothing else but those things, would she not learn math, reading, writing, botany and hand skills? And yet we've been brought up to think, "Oh yes, those sound great. We'll do them. Someday. After we do a couple of pages of phonics and math. And handwriting. If we have time...."

SLOW SCHOOLING

Habits and appetites are also cultivated during those young years. If we spend too much time away from our homes, children learn that home is simply a place to collect our material goods and lay down our heads, that it is not a place of production and enterprise. If we involve our children in too many classes, cultural events, vacations and sports teams, they will learn to persistently seek to be entertained or overwork to seek that elusive gold and fickle public and cultural approval. If we do not involve them in the real honest-to-goodness "real world" of laundry, cooking, and daily mundane chores, they will learn to be passive and expect to be served. If we put too much emphasis on academics, they will find it normal to amass tremendous student loans for the sake of having multiple letters after their names but have no practical outworking of what it means to use

THE REAL WORLD

their knowledge to love and serve others, much less how to survive with basic skills.

I'd encourage you to consider what your "real world" involves, and if the journey your children are on reflect that. Too many of us are floating (or riding the rapids!) down the years of the rest of our lives without giving any consideration to our own talents, interests, gifts and desires. Instead, we are trapped within a system in which sameness is encouraged and sometimes demanded. We are, at this time, expected to fall in line to mass schooling, to cultural thought and behaviors, to join and celebrate the "real world" of taking on debts of all kinds, living a consumer lifestyle, and always, always pushing forward to get the next new thing or upgrade. We don't know our neighbors, we're seeking our affirmations on online media platforms, and we're living in a world of virtual-everything. That, to me, doesn't sound very "real" at all.

BLOG
"Goodbye, Self-Confidence; Hello, Trust"
Tuesday, May 20, 2008, 05:58pm

> There is more to learning than just acquiring a checkmark in someone else's idea of a scope and sequence for a child's age (or "grade"). I need to remember: Isaiah 54:13, "And all thy children shall be taught of the LORD; and great shall be the peace of thy children."
>
> When the Lord leads me to teaching materials, textbooks or otherwise,

THE REAL WORLD

I need to just trust Him in that leading and not allow doubts to germinate into the fear that I am not doing "enough." Jesus Himself (and His leading) is more than enough, even in our schooling. And if I hold fast to that, great shall be my peace, too.

3

WHAT SLOW SCHOOLING IS NOT

The idea of "slow schooling" is not new, but it sometimes gets confused with other ideas such as "unschooling." Unschooling is defined as "allowing children as much freedom to learn in the world, as their parents can comfortably bear."[1] John Holt and his followers are careful to explain that this is not "un-parenting," but say that their children (and by definition, students) learn only what and when it makes sense for them to do so. This is different from

SLOW SCHOOLING

what I term "slow schooling," especially from a Christian perspective.

The scriptures are clear that parents are responsible for their child's upbringing, and that includes not only their care and protection, but their education as well. I realize that Deuteronomy 6:5-9 has been the clarion call to bring Christian parents into submission regarding teaching their children at home, but it's hard to grasp the entirety of "And thou shalt love the LORD thy God with all thine heart, and with all thy soul, and with all thy might.. And these words, which I command thee this day, shall be in thine heart: And thou shalt teach them diligently unto thy children, and shalt talk of them when thou sittest in thine house, and when thou walkest by the way, and when thou liest down, and when thou risest up. And thou shalt bind them for a sign upon thine

WHAT SLOW SCHOOLING is **NOT**

hand, and they shall be as frontlets between thine eyes. And thou shalt write them upon the posts of thy house, and on thy gates" (Deut 6:5-9) and then run with it like you've got the football and a set of fire jets on your sneakers. Yes, parents—and fathers, especially—are expected to raise and nurture their children in the admonition of the Lord, but with regards to by who and by what means your child may learn algebra...that seems to be an issue that can only be settled within each individual family. Slow schooling, therefore, is not an ordained biblical method of educating your children. Practically speaking, however, a child spending the enormity of their day under the tutelage of other people in alternative systems will not easily abandon the implicit worldviews they are taught five or more days a week. One hour of Sunday school at the local church, and even the short time in the evenings of family time, is no match for the weekly average of 32 hours in their seats at the public school, and to insist otherwise is rather disingenuous.

Because parents are ultimately responsible for their child's education, whether at home or elsewhere, parents do bear the burden of choosing and selecting opportunities for learning. That is to say, yes, the child may have an innate interest in botanical flowers, but if the child is never exposed to the wonders of chemistry, that child may never reach the potentially satisfying work of pharmacognosy or phytotherapy. Or even know what those words are without an introduction to Latin. Parents, with their experience and wisdom can, and should, provide at least a clear direction for their children to embark upon, even as they take into account individual and unique interests and proclivities.

WHAT SLOW SCHOOLING is **NOT**

Slow schooling is not full-time child management. It is not scheduling the child for every hour of the day or week. It is not marching the child from one subject to another to chore time to lunch time to naptime to story time ad nauseam. Yes, it allows routine in the day for meals and so forth, but it also allows plenty of time for boredom and personal interests and projects. It also does not necessarily demand the completion of activities or even curriculum for which the child shows no interest or inclination. Many subjects are simply imposed simply because the child is a certain age (or "grade" level) and have no bearing on whether or not the child is ready to undertake the study.

Slow schooling is also not "school at home." Unless this is a customary practice in home life, we don't begin our days with the Pledge of

SLOW SCHOOLING

Allegiance or sit in rows. Rather, education is entwined into the fiber and fabric of our days, not as an addendum or necessarily separate. Just as a mother may sit on the sofa knitting up a sweater, a child may be taking apart the last computer gadget at the dining room table. It is not considered "home economics time" for mother any more than "electronics period" for the child. Routines may, again, be in play; we might generally read aloud during a certain portion of the day for example. But flexibility allows for steeping tea for the neighbor at the door should that occur. Math work one day may entail a full and engrossed 90 minutes and not be seen again for days. The routine, more loosely defined than a schedule, is our helper and never our master.

Although children who are homeschooled are generally well-mannered and excel in

WHAT SLOW SCHOOLING is **NOT**

socialization across all people ages and groups, the goal of slow schooling is not to "raise good kids." Instead, we endeavor to raise children to live with a full understanding, and hopefully a sincere and precious faith, that works itself out by the Holy Spirit in growing them in character, deeds, and charity. Behavior modification is never the goal or the means by which to achieve that. In all things, from making the bed to showing kindness to a sibling to putting forth an honest effort and willingness into whatever is attempted, there is a view of the cross and a treasured gratitude for the love that God has in His mercy lavished upon them. Humility, and not self-esteem, is the real prize.

Lastly, slow schooling is not in an effort to impress the outside world with our virtuoso violinists or early college entrances or impressive standardized test scores. It is, rather, an obedient

SLOW SCHOOLING

call to the Lord who tenderly draws the conscience and heart to a more present, quiet, simple, and deliberate lifestyle. It may not be the answer or road for everyone, but for me and my house, the pilgrimage has been pleasant.

4

WHAT SLOW SCHOOLING IS

BLOG

"The One Thing That Matters"

Friday, January 25, 2008, 07:27am

> I know it is not within my power to choose for my children the path they will take when they are of age. And yet, they are currently entrusted to me. Will I give more thought to their clothing and physical health than to their spiritual wellbeing? Will I be

SLOW SCHOOLING

> satisfied they ate their vegetables even if their Bible was not cracked open this day?

If we now know what slow schooling is NOT, then what IS it? Slow schooling IS about putting priorities in proper ordering, and purposes to put feet to the intangible and ever eluding desires of our soul. For Christians, the wrenching cry of our hearts is for our children to come to repentance and salvation through the Lord Jesus Christ, and everything else either streams from that very thought or else leads right back to it. Where we lose our footing is in trying to consider, "...and this is how this is accomplished...."

WHAT SLOW SCHOOLING IS

Salvation is from God alone, but that fact does not excuse us from the responsibilities—no, the unparalleled joy—in not only teaching our children the gospel, but in living it out in tangible ways in everyday life. Naturally, we fail at times in our endeavors, but the trajectory of our years and the witness others see ought to be an obvious growth in holiness and in a humble trust for God in the circumstances He has either lovingly chastened us with or allowed to sanctify us.

Thus, schooling at home, and slow schooling specifically, endeavors to seek first the kingdom of God. There are many practical outworkings we can point to, of which none ought to be done with a spirit of legalism or steeped in a pseudo-holy moralism. Instead, because we cherish Jesus Christ as precious to our souls, we long for others to know Him also. This fervent desire is compounded by maternal or paternal love for the children in our care.

Prayerlessness is unthinkable for our children. Prayer daily for each child, for their salvation, for their growth, for any concerns or struggles there may be, can only be carried by the humble parent who understands that in all things, God is sovereign. God's sovereignty is not an excuse not to pick up the armor we have been fitted for. Children seeing a parent in prayer, as well as hearing open prayers, learn not only the seriousness of living under a righteous God, but get to know His compassionate and lovingkindness as well when prayers are "coincidentally" answered.

Reading, and learning, the Holy Bible is also a key part of the slow schooling day. There was a time when our culture was quite literate in

WHAT SLOW SCHOOLING IS

the scriptures, saint and sinner alike, and today we still use many proverbs and words borrowed from there in our everyday speech. Bible literacy among Christians today is appalling. There is a vast difference between revering the Bible and reading it, and Albert Mohler rightly quips, "We will not believe more than we know, and we will not live higher than our beliefs."[1] Understanding this Book and recognizing and seeing that it is ALL about Jesus, from Genesis to Revelation, is unequivocally what is most needed for any child to grow in wisdom and godliness. Furthermore, it relates the history of the world that has never been refuted by either science or archeological evidence. Not knowing the Bible is a great hinderance to life.

Slow schooling encourages the child to walk in the footprints of their parents. This is, of

SLOW SCHOOLING

course, a stumbling block to many who think they are not well equipped to wear the boots their sons will want to later put on (we'll address being qualified to teach in chapter 6). In any list you could possibly jot for the good of your children: to be happy, to love God, to serve others, to bring out their unique qualities...you must be the forerunner. Do you desire your child to love learning? Then, you must love learning as well. Do you desire your child to learn to run an orderly home? Then, you must endeavor to do likewise. The adverse, of course, is also true. If you desire your children to treat others with lovingkindness or to eschew gossip, then you must display those qualities as well. Cotton Mather once said, "Except you do yourselves walk in the way of the Lord, you will be very careless about bringing your children to such a walk." Hypocrites do not raise the kinds of

WHAT SLOW SCHOOLING **IS**

children they demand they become by their words.

Slow schooling not only allows for ministry and service to others, it is the heart of the home. In the ebb and flow of the day, we learn to love one another by reading to a sibling, or allowing for the interruption of either a 4 year old wanting to "help" prepare a meal or a neighbor that stops by. For our family, it means we answer our telephone when it rings and open the door when there's a knock.

Because character drives habit and practice, it is something we concern ourselves with in our slow school. You may be able to force a child to complete a year of US history, but if he isn't humble enough to see himself in the broader context of what God is doing through nations, he not only won't care about your history

SLOW SCHOOLING

lessons, he will miss the obvious lessons that will continue throughout his lifetime as he sees (or, doesn't see) how a nation rises and falls according to their responses to God and to His people.[2] And, of course, what happens in his own country will in due course affect him and his life greatly. So discipline is kindly meted out as needed, and repentance and restoration is expected. Forgiveness, concern for others, and a sound work ethic has its beginnings in the humble home.

Slow schooling is, by deliberation, slow. "In Genesis Adam and Eve took what looked like a shortcut to receive knowledge, and he gave up the relationship he had with God. Satan has never forgotten that man tends to sacrifice relationship with knowledge."[3] Unfortunately, we are still sons of Adam and daughters of Eve[4] and today we are still sacrificing

WHAT SLOW SCHOOLING IS

opportunities to cultivate relationships with our children for the alluring promises of moving up in the world by way of grade point averages and completed academic courses. We'll address how "complete" those courses really are in chapter 5.

In making decisions regarding the education of our children, endeavoring to equip them with a biblical worldview ought to be front and center, secondary to all else. When the vast numbers of professing Christians believe things that are either simply not true or, at worst, blasphemous, we ought to be sober minded in considering our ways in everything in which we have some semblance of choice.[5] What may sound like common sense or feel reasonable in the current day of educating our children—whether away in another setting or even at home—we must remain vigilant to an eternal perspective.

BLOG
"Education of a Sheeple"
Wednesday, April 30, 2007, 04:03pm

I don't know. Maybe I'm wrong. But when I am an old woman, I am going to have fond memories of my daughter baking banana bread, my son building elaborate Lego creations, my two young daughters "reading" piles of books on their beds, and the baby chasing after balls that tease across the floor. Education is not the totality of life; it is a tool that is honed and polished as we walk along the way with our children, discipling

WHAT SLOW SCHOOLING **IS**

them and teaching them what is truly important. All we like sheep have gone astray, but it is so good to find the narrow gate by which the Shepherd calls. And it doesn't take a PhD.

5

Why Not Government Schooling?

BLOG

"Three More Reasons to Homeschool"

Monday, June 30, 2008, 09:10am

1. Reading
2. Writing
3. Arithmetic

SLOW SCHOOLING

When I was a child, I LOVED everything about going to school. I loved my teachers, my college-ruled notebook paper, homework, and peers. I was bored out of my mind during the summer and spent much of it trying to convince my little brother that playing school was not only fun, but actually very necessary. I couldn't wait to go shopping with "The List" that I needed for school: full-size, nick-free pencils that smelled sharply of cedar; crease-free Crayola boxes; scissors that didn't stick; and oh! that paste! My memories of schooling are mostly positive, and I was a good girl who not only did all her homework, but sought out the Student of the Month awards, which I won multiple times.

All my memories of my education are just that: childhood memories...that have not only filtered out the negatives, they didn't even

WHY NOT GOVERNMENT SCHOOLING

realize that certain aspects of my schooling were negative. Later, as I began to teach elementary students, I began to understand how much I had missed. I also saw that even by the fourth grade, many of my students had already been funneled into the different statum of "good" students, "below grade level" students, and "behavioral problem" students. I also saw that it was near impossible to change those classifications, and that in every circumstance, attentive and loving parenting in a safe and happy home about guaranteed the success of any student. It was never a matter of having the most experienced amazing teacher (and there were—and are—plenty of them!); the foundation was—and is—involved and concerned parents.

Presumably, the reader IS an involved and concerned parent. Moreover, the reader

SLOW SCHOOLING

probably already has a good deal of doubts or misgivings regarding the appropriateness or profits of government schooling, so perhaps much of what is in this chapter will come as no surprise. However, full disclosure seems to lack forthcoming in what a "public education" really entails in all of its glory, and my desire is to simply point them out.

To begin with, classes by design have a lot of students. Most have between 22 to 34 students, but let us begin by supposing the class your child will be entering into has 12. Perchance, you are excited about this, because the teacher-to-student ratio is so low, that you know your child will get all the attention he needs. The truth is that your child will still be one of twelve children, even if he is involved in an alternative multi-age program. I know you feel overwhelmed at times, thinking, "I can

WHY NOT GOVERNMENT SCHOOLING

hardly handle the ONE five-year-old I have," but have you honestly weighed the enormity of the task to care for, teach and train TWELVE small children all at once? Why do you believe a starry-eyed 23-year-old, fresh out of college with no mothering experience, would better meet your child's academic, social and emotional needs not only better than you, but with eleven other children pulling upon her skirts?

The reality, from my short experience as a government school teacher, is not any different from the experience from the gentleman I know who has served in the system for almost 40 years.

If your Suzy is a good girl, a sweet girl, one who loves her teacher and does her best, she will receive warm smiles and awards. Her

SLOW SCHOOLING

report cards will be glowing. I'd be surprised if she ever got a hug from her teacher (especially if he were a male), given the environment of trepidation over abuse charges. If she is quiet, she will be largely ignored, relegated to the back row because the teacher needs to give her attention to the rowdy children who will sit up front and center. Suzy may spend time in a room with her head down for 15 minute spells, because certain other children misbehaved to the point of bringing the teacher to frustration. She won't be able to read her teacher as well as she reads you, and at some point may get a stern rebuke that was inappropriate. She will try to tell you her side of things, but...you weren't there...so you'll need to take sides (hers or the teacher?). She will want to be liked, and although students and teachers will give her their approval, peers with strong leadership

WHY NOT GOVERNMENT SCHOOLING

personalities, for good or bad, will draw her like a magnet.

Perhaps what you have is a Sam. Sam is a normal, all-out boy. He is the one that jumps out of bed to dive into the peanut butter jar, and makes carpet-ring tracks around your sofa as he pours out fire truck wails from his lips. If you send Sam to school, he will be expected to SIT DOWN. The best you can hope for is that he will have not only a teacher, but one every single year that will understand him and keep him moving: running errands, hall passes, passing out papers, gathering supplies. But, alas, that would be unfair to the other children not to have their turns, so he must SIT DOWN and STAY THERE. And the request made upon this will not be made with eyes full of an eager teacher's understanding and hope past the first day of school. Trying to restrain Sam will be

SLOW SCHOOLING

like trying to get a baby tiger to sit in an invisible cage for hours at a time, and then sending it a taser shock when it moves. Meetings with you will be made, and after a multiple of behavior contracts and positive/negative reward systems come and go, you may become presented with the choice of drugging your baby, or sending him to a special needs classroom. You know, however, that all he really needs are short 15 minute segments of bookwork interspersed with 45 minutes of run-around play and chores time, and that in those short spurts he will learn. A lot, in fact.

It will take the average child 25 minutes to do a simple handwriting task. It will take 40 minutes to get through a math page. Three minutes to get everyone's attention and five minutes to get into a line, if everyone

WHY NOT GOVERNMENT SCHOOLING

(including Sam) is cooperating. Suzy will spend a lot of time just waiting. So will Doreen, Eric, Justin and Chelsea. Waiting to begin. Waiting for everyone to catch up to everyone else. Waiting for the class to give the teacher their "eyes and ears." Waiting for the story to begin. Waiting for the teacher to begin. Waiting for recess to get here. Waiting, already, for the last day of school. It is because of all of this waste of time that students need to give time to afterschool homework, despite having already spent five or six hours in the classroom.

Study materials will not be geared to your child. As much as the teacher wants to individualize instruction, that can only go so far. I sometimes joke with my husband that I had a more difficult time teaching because I was trying to "homeschool" each of my 34 students before I even knew what homeschooling was. In

SLOW SCHOOLING

the typical classroom, some children will just fall through the proverbial crack, and it may take four teachers before Cindy gets her spellings lists off the SAT prep guides, which is where she is at. Teachers don't worry too much about this though, because at the end of the year, if they are at all mulling over disappointments in scholastic achievements, they all have hope that "the next teacher" will succeed.

Teachers for the most part will listen to you and share with you a desire to help your child reach the stars. But it will be all on their terms, and if you have a problem with a book, a program, an assembly (and, oh boy, there are a LOT of them), it will be just that: your problem. You will get head nodding and understanding if you don't want your kindergartner to learn about condoms, but eyes will roll and tongues will wag about you in the teachers' lounge.

WHY NOT GOVERNMENT SCHOOLING

And your five year old will still learn about condoms. Your child has ceased to be yours, even if you are the president of the PTA. This will dawn on you in a whole new way when you try to help your child with her homework, but your help won't be good enough because "it's not how the teacher does it." Parents generally have a great respect for teachers and their training, but years of sitting in the lounge at lunch have taught me that the feeling, unfortunately, is not mutual.

The curriculum seems to change with the winds of culture. Reading, writing, and arithmetic are not the foundational blocks, as evidenced by the growing need for remediation even at the collegiate level where one in four students find themselves in (and paying for) classes such as Basic English or Basic Math.[1] These are, presumably, students who were at a

SLOW SCHOOLING

certain academic level just to gain acceptance into "higher education." Unfortunately, that academic level of scholarship continues to decline as evidenced by standardized testing, and the reasons leaders in the industry seem to come up with are weak at best: the focus on teacher quality,[2] the quantity of tests students are required to take,[3] the economy, or immigrant children.[4] The best scenario, they say, is to give it time. What they don't explain is why, even if a child learns to read, the complexity of the language and vocabulary has continued in decline in the last two hundred years plus,[5] still plainly evidenced by lay folk today simply by comparing current newspapers and text from those of a hundred years ago. I have even heard the King James Bible is "too difficult to understand", but the Flesch-Kincaid research company's grade level indicator placed it at an average grade of 5.8,[6] requiring less

WHY NOT GOVERNMENT SCHOOLING

comprehension than the current USA Today newspaper.[7]

Another reason children may not be meeting their academic potential may have to do with the fact that schools are also spending time teaching them how to be salespeople instead (or, rather, recruiting their mothers to be salespeople for them). Just a simple Google search for "fundraising school assemblies" turned up more than a million hits,[8] and from the look of things, far more were concerned with how to turn principals into clowns or who to hire in order to rake in more money for the school. I cannot simply understand how a system can garner more than $9000 in tax money per student on average and still cannot somehow afford to buy schoolbooks, computers, and swing sets.[9] As a teacher, I hated marching my students during their writing

SLOW SCHOOLING

workshop times to gather for assemblies where hired entertainers tried to whip everyone up in a frenzy to sell $5000 worth of overpriced goods no one needed in order to win a $15 boombox. And as a taxpayer, I'm appalled.

Now, when I was in kindergarten in 1975, I don't recall a lot of assemblies. But I do remember cutting out barns from red construction paper, dressing up as a butterfly, taking naptime on a cot, and finding myself enveloped in the hugs of my teacher who smelled like ivory soap. By the time I was teaching kindergarten, naptime was long gone, five-year-olds were expected to read before spring, and hugging was taboo. More recent developments include story times that are now going to involve more than Dr. Seuss. Books that promote traditional family units are now discouraged at best (banned at worst),

WHY NOT GOVERNMENT SCHOOLING

including anything that can be "perceived" as being discriminatory, up to and including references to "mom" and "dad" or "husband" and "wife." What this means, in essence, is that if a teacher reads a book with a traditional family unit ("traditional" in the sense of more than 6000 years of human history across every culture in the entire world), he or she will need to also read a book that highlights an "alternative."

What is the necessity of introducing topics to children that are hardly beyond learning letter sounds and counting beans? Well, as Adolf Hitler said in 1922, "When an opponent declares, 'I will not come over to your side,' I say calmly, 'Your child belongs to us already. What are you? You will pass on. Your descendants, however, now stand in the new camp. In a

SLOW SCHOOLING

short time they will know nothing but this new community.'"[10]

The issue is not simply teaching about topics that parents may not agree with or even endorse at any age in an arena outside of their own family and faith, it is the forceful and persuasive instruction from a mindset that denigrates parental authority to the point of not allowing parents to even opt out of sessions that they deem inappropriate for their own children.[11]

There is no respect for hunger, sniffles, or fatigue. I'm not real sure that "snack time" exists anymore, and school lunches still are not as healthy as they need to be for a child getting so many of their calories there. A healthy school lunch would consist of quality protein and fats for starters, but doing so would be cost-prohibitive and a losing battle with the

WHY NOT GOVERNMENT SCHOOLING

offerings by the fast food businesses already embedded into the schools. Even if a parent were to provide a healthy sack lunch, trading (or tossing) is not an art lost on the young. A case of the sniffles might get a smidge of sympathy, but it won't be served with tea and a smile. And even though a child's natural rhythm is to slow down and regroup in the afternoon (especially sometime between 2 and 4pm), many children are pushed to more extracurricular activities after school.

Perhaps you are thinking that the school needs your child, that your child has professed Jesus and that out of deep-felt concern for the lost you ought to send her to proclaim Him. I find this to be rather incredulous unless the family is accustomed to openly witnessing to people in the open air. Unless there has been a great deal of role modeling, a five-year-old or

SLOW SCHOOLING

even a fifteen-year-old is generally not going to speak freely about spiritual matters, even if they were allowed to do so. Graduation prayers, witnessing, and even passing out tracts is strongly discouraged; recently, a deputy showed up to warn a 7-year-old to stop sharing the Bible verses his mother had put into his lunch box.[12] Think of a child in a classroom who is pressed and chided by the teacher she SO loves. Why would that child not be one of the majority to abandon the faith by her sophomore year in college?[13] To assume or even hope that a Christian child in a staunch secular school system will not only overcome the pressure to quit Christ, but in the process convert a mass of peers, is hopelessly naive, or choosing to be ignorant of the tragic facts.

Lastly, there is a great temptation to blend even independent homeschooling with

WHY NOT GOVERNMENT SCHOOLING

alternative "school-at-home" programs (which, legally speaking, means a homeschool is no longer considered "independent"). Virtual schools and parent partnership programs promise and provide funds for curriculum, computers, outside lessons, in exchange for...something. That something, however, is insidious, and the price won't necessarily be paid for by our own children, but by our children's children. Once there are enough homeschoolers enrolled, the state will look to impose more regulations upon what homeschoolers can do to be eligible for the (at that point, decreasing) cash allotments. In the end, children still end up belonging to the government school system. Such is the challenge now in Alaska,[14] and ought to be a warning bell to families.

SLOW SCHOOLING

I'm reminded of Numbers 11:4-6:

> And the mixt multitude that was among them fell a lusting: and the children of Israel also wept again, and said, Who shall give us flesh to eat? [Or computers to use? Or math workbooks? Or music lessons?] We remember the fish, [ready lesson plans] which we did eat in Egypt freely ["free" with your tax dollars]; the cucumbers, and the melons, and the leeks, and the onions, and the garlick, [bulletin boards, projector screens, multitude of science equipment]: but now our soul is dried away: there is nothing at all, beside this manna,[nothing but this Bible] before our eyes.

What do you really need to home educate? A Bible, paper and pencils, life skills, and the great outdoors. But God is gracious, and He does provide even the lesser things. I recall deciding that my children ought to learn an instrument

WHY NOT GOVERNMENT SCHOOLING

of some kind, mainly because I had not. When my then five-year-old daughter requested to learn to play a violin (a violin?!), I asked around and discovered a lovely group of volunteers that were teaching homeschooled children all sorts of stringed instruments, for $1.50 a week, with a $15 a month instrument rental. If the funds are not there to provide your child for whatever your family deems necessary for their education, I would encourage you to first ask (Matthew 7:11), and second to accept whatever the answer as the most wise. Plenty of families I personally know have been blessed with all manner of provision, and there is no real reason why a child of God ought to look to the state before kneeling before his or her Father first.

It may be overwhelming to think of keeping your child home. Maybe you don't think you

SLOW SCHOOLING

can teach math. Maybe you don't even WANT to. I know you have a list of projects you cannot wait to delve into without children wanting to take over your lap with storybooks. But, dear Christian mother or father, consider this: 100 years from now when you are gone to that place of glory, the legacy of what you have sown will reap a hundredfold. I would encourage you to pick up your Bible, glean from Him what is truly important, and have the courage and quiet strength it will take to pull your baby closer to your side as you both watch the yellow school bus pass your home sweet home by.

Is sending your child to a government school a sin? I don't rightly know, but at the least it seems unwise. But if it is to be, let it be a rare and tragic situation that makes their attendance a temporary exception for all involved.

6

On Being "Qualified" to Teach

BLOG

"The TEST: Are You Competent to Homeschool?"
Sunday, April 27, 2008, 05:02pm

> "You don't have to go to college to get a degree in education. (In fact, that degree might prove to be counterproductive because education programs prepare you to teach how the state wants you to teach.) You don't have to have teachers in your family

SLOW SCHOOLING

background. Nor is it necessary that you were once the teacher's pet, or are an expert in clapping erasers. The test is rather simple to take. It should take only a few minutes, and then you will know.

The first thing you do is wait until it is late at night. Then, very quietly, go from room to room in your house. Peek in carefully, and see if you find any sleeping children. Then be sure that these are your own children. If there are wee ones in your home during the wee hours, and if they belong to you, you are competent to homeschool. The true Expert on education is the very One who gave you these children."

> — from *When You Rise Up*,
> by R.C. Sproul Jr.

ON BEING "QUALIFIED" to TEACH

And again, I will put my trust in him. And again, Behold I and the children which God hath given me (Hebrews 2:13).

When people learn that I am homeschooling our children, the most common response I get goes something like this: "Oh, YOU can do that because you (went to college...were once a teacher...have a lot of patience...)." The underlying assumption is that my higher education and/or teaching experiences in the public schools adequately prepared me to embrace the endeavor of home educating. Nothing could be further from the truth, and it is unfortunate that my experiences have tagged me as someone out of touch with the reality of how "hard" it is to homeschool.

SLOW SCHOOLING

Homeschooling, and certainly slow schooling, is not about adopting the government school's means and methods of transferring knowledge and using behavioral modification in an attempt to raise a moral people. We ought to, rather, be profoundly grateful for the differences, because it is rather apparent public schools have not accomplished their own goals in these objectives, no matter how much tax money they throw at the system.

Qualifying to teach our own children is not a matter of educational attainments, licensure, or experience. And it is most certainly not a matter of permission. The deeper issue at the root is authority. The question we need to ask ourselves is, where is the responsibility for the child's wellbeing and education supposed to reside? When a couple conceives a child, who has the authority to choose where the child lives

ON BEING "QUALIFIED" to TEACH

or what the child wears and eats? Our answers to these questions of authority are the rudders for a child's education and upbringing, and for human flourishing as a whole.

Granted, new parents are hesitant and unsure. They must learn to nurse, change diapers, and tune into routines and feedings and naptimes. They must learn to discern between distressed cries for comfort and whining for sugar snacks. But no one is better motivated to learn how to make that discernment and learn those coping skills because of their investment with their child. No one will love that child more.

My hope is that readers here are not dealing with catastrophic situations. More likely, the dismissal of home schooling is due to a lack of confidence, unfortunately fed by the state and

SLOW SCHOOLING

media and culture at large. Educating your own child is not contingent upon your confidence, experience, training, or abilities. Those qualities don't even guarantee or secure the success of children in any school system. It equates to one thing: You Care.

If you didn't care, you wouldn't celebrate your child's first step (no curriculum needed). If you didn't care, you wouldn't worry about your child's first tummy ache (chicken soup...check...). If you didn't care, you certainly wouldn't be reading a book and considering alternative ways of educating your child. What you need to realize is that for all of your child's life, you HAVE been educating your child already. From the very first cuddle, you've taught your child that you were (or weren't) available, that you did (or didn't) love him or her, and that your rules and expectations were (or weren't)

ON BEING "QUALIFIED" to TEACH

expected to be met and followed. In fact, you've been teaching your child his or her entire life.

Why do we forget this? Or discount it? Oh, sure, your baby learned to walk...but he won't learn to read?? I once had a sweet mother visit my home because she wanted to "pick my brain" about schooling their special needs child along with the daughter they had already brought home. The child in question came home every day from the government school with not only stomach aches, but cards decrying her misbehavior: not finishing her work in the allotted time. I asked, "Instead of waiting for June (an arbitrary time of when learning "stops" for the summer), why don't you pull her out now?" Incredibly, this mom was elated! She knew in her heart it was the right thing to do but needed the encouragement and assurance

SLOW SCHOOLING

from someone else who was not part of the system.

You don't need someone else's permission or assurance.

Except, for the most part, now you do.

Because ever since we agreed that the state had a more vested interest in our children than we do, we now need to get that permission or approval to do the very natural act of educating our own children if they are in a particular age group. This was, again, not due to the fact that home educated children are failing in test scores, life experiences, socialization, work, or cultural or community involvement. This was due to, again, the wrong answer to the question of authority. Where is

ON BEING "QUALIFIED" to TEACH

the responsibility for the child's wellbeing and education supposed to reside? But here we are.

If you decide to home educate your child, whether it via slow schooling or the most regimented of academic pursuits, you will need to obey the government and fulfill whatever requirements your state has set for the privilege of raising your own in this way. Some states are fairly liberal, not requiring any information whatsoever, and others are quite draconian, demanding parents hold certificates or turn in hours as proof of schooling. In any case, not only is it your responsibility to follow the law, doing so protects the rights of other parents to continue in their own educational endeavors with their own children.

You are not incompetent to educate your children. There is, in fact, NO evidence to

SLOW SCHOOLING

suggest that a parent who has dropped out of high school is less qualified to teach their child than a school official with a multitude of letters after their name.[1] Teacher qualifications do not make for better students, and demanding certification or curriculum approval is not only unreasonable, it is an affront to parents everywhere. The reason I can educate my child is the same reason you have: you're the parent. Understanding that alone will grow you in confidence and courage. Embrace it.

"That best academy, a mother's knee."

— James Russell Lowell

"One good mother is worth a hundred schoolmasters."

— George Herbert

7

Equipping and Caring for the Teacher

BLOG

"A Simple Life"

Monday, February 19, 2007, 03:10pm

It is exasperating, excruciating, exhausting work to be a mother. But all things considered, it really is a simple life: love God, love your husband, love your children, keep the home. This is a life full enough, and anything else looms to threaten and steal

SLOW SCHOOLING

precious emotional, mental, and physical strength from the limited time we really have to live. Someday, perhaps, my great-great-grand-daughter will wipe her brow, put the children to nap, and wonder about me, about how I "did it." I will tell her, "not as well as I wanted, nor as much as I had hoped, but Jesus walked with me through it all, and that was more than enough."

At this point, even with a decision and a commitment to home educate, the reality of such an endeavor sets in: who will do it? Simply asking the question, however, reveals the starting point: the starting point that says, "Children will not learn without an educator."

EQUIPPING and CARING for the TEACHER

The fact is, children are learning all the time, even within the cozy confines of the womb. Granted, they may be learning lessons you wished weren't so intriguing or harmful, or they may be avoiding the harder and more satisfying pursuits of endeavoring to attempt new things, but they ARE learning.

In America's post-industrial culture today, women are typically the homemakers and educators for the family. This is true, even if those women have outside careers to attend. Once home, they are thinking of meals, or laundry, or of dental appointments that need making. One could argue quite convincingly, women were created to be nurturers, but even without a Biblical worldview, that is the gender that tends to oversee those tasks. Therefore, in this chapter I am going to address a topic that I have experience with: equipping and caring for

SLOW SCHOOLING

the mother who is home educating. Men reading this chapter may find helps for themselves if they are the primary teacher, but I am certain that reading this will enable them to better support their wives in the endeavor.

Home educating mothers need to know everything that was discussed in the previous chapter, and know it by heart as well as by head: you do not need to be trained to teach your children. That being said, just like any other pursuit, gaining knowledge of the variety of methods gives a mother a plethora of tools to best meet each child's unique needs. One child may love the structure of having a list of quality literature books to read; another child simply needs a library card and full access.

So how do you know what means to employ in educating an individual child? At

EQUIPPING and CARING for the TEACHER

best you find a friendly and encouraging mentor who has many years of homeschooling accomplished. This mentor would have children who are a delight to be around, who are friendly, curious, and observant. They have an answer to "What are you reading these days?" or "What projects have you been working on lately?" This mentor also would look like she gets plenty of sleep, and would rarely answer "How are you?" with a frazzled "Crazy busy!" If there is anyone within your sphere of community who looks like she may be of help, by all means take her out for a latte and humbly ask for a little ongoing help and support.

Homeschooling conferences are another way to get equipping and encouragement, many with online streaming. However, remember that homeschooling has become one big and

SLOW SCHOOLING

growing business, and expect to be inundated with a veritable flood (and I do mean flood) of curriculum choices that all promise to give your student (and you) the education of everyone's dreams. Also remember that every author (including me!) and every speaker brings their worldview into whatever they are saying or selling. If you are interested in slow schooling, a jam packed curriculum that hits all eight subjects within a single school year isn't going to deliver what you want, no matter how wonderful the product looks. I suggest taking the time to write down questions you would like an answer to, or particular needs that you have, BEFORE you attend any conference. That way, you can return to your list and reorient your purpose there as often as necessary.

There are many online and in-person classes available for the homeschooling parent now. If

EQUIPPING and CARING for the TEACHER

you sense your child might need help with understanding math concepts, you may find tutoring via technology either for your child or for yourself. Let go of the idea that you must have a firm grasp on any subject you find needful or your child finds interesting. That is part of the learning process: how to find out what you want to know via a means that you can understand.

Likewise, there are many curriculum helps and even scheduling tools. Cautions are in order for these as well, as many of them can become unintentional tyrants. If you choose to use a timeline or a schedule of some sort, please remember that these are not your masters, but your servants. These can be excellent helps to encourage orderliness, but the danger is using them to the detriment of flexibility and, in

SLOW SCHOOLING

failing to follow them perfectly, becomes seeds of discontent and discouragement.

Slow schooling in general needs few tools:
- materials (such as Bibles, books, paper and pencils)
- time (to think, to plan the next nature hike, to read aloud)
- space (to store supplies and to draw and to lounge with a book).

Keep it simple.

Keeping it simple is a very easy way to avoid the classic "burnout" that can occur in homeschooling mamas. Also, it is good to remember your "why." WHY are your homeschooling? WHY does slow schooling interest you? Is it to build a better relationship

EQUIPPING and CARING for the TEACHER

with your children? If so, then you will keep it simple by limiting the amount of classes or sports teams your child joins. You do not have to account for every minute of their day with some flavor of schoolwork or chore, either. It is good to maintain perspective on the greater view of what you are doing: preparing an adult to be godly and to love the Lord. Keep the broader, eternal story front of mind when things feel overwhelming, and start cutting back as needed to get back to "simple."

It is also helpful to respect natural ebbs and flows throughout the day, week, and seasons. Perhaps you accomplish a roaring great deal of housework by lunchtime, but your afternoon is slow and marked by rows of knitting. Your child, on the other hand, may be very slow to start but, like a Mack Truck, picks up speed as the day goes on. Perhaps most of your winter is

SLOW SCHOOLING

taken up with read alouds, but your summers are full of nature studies. You may have requirements for reading assignments, but slow schooling allows for flexibility with regards to when it gets done. We all have habits and preferences on how and where to work. Certainly you can aid or assist your child in making changes as needed, but remember to give your child grace in making those changes. Remember also to give that grace to yourself, as you venture into new efforts, whatever they may be.

Please be wary of the comparison trap. That is the trap of having in mind either a version or even a particular method of how your home education program will look. With so many other parents homeschooling, it is easy to look at their children, their homes, their curriculum choices...and wonder why your decisions aren't

EQUIPPING and CARING for the TEACHER

matching up OR why theirs aren't as fruitful. The see-saw of despair-pride can be nauseating. Your self-worth is not found in your child's standardized test scores. It may be comforting to know where your child is contrast to another child in growth or academic pursuits, but better would be to ask questions like: "Is he growing in holiness? How is his character changing? Does he love learning? What does he need next?"

Lastly (before we get to the list!), pursue your OWN learning. If you desire for your child a lifelong love of learning and study and growth, then you must do the same. Our behavior, as always, proves our beliefs. If it is not important to us to read or write, it will likely seem pointless to our children as well. What are YOU interested in learning? The best secret of home schooling is that education is for everyone, not only the child.

SLOW SCHOOLING

To end our chapter, here is a list of ideas to think about in equipping and caring for a homeschooling mama to have the strength and endurance for the race that is before her to educate her children:

- in the morning, prepare your heart (prayer and Bible), your body (get dressed), and evening (make your bed and think about supper)
- watch out for time spent on social media; cull if needed
- pay attention to your, and your child's, physical and mental states
- expect to be frustrated and discouraged at times!
- eat regular, wholesome, real food, meals
- make time for an outing with a friend

EQUIPPING and CARING for the TEACHER

- create a routine or schedule
- limit the amount of outside activities
- keep hydrated
- remember your "why"
- protect the family meal time
- have a time of quiet rest or reading every day
- your children are not interruptions
- take a field trip within your own town
- do something different, like read aloud under the apple tree outside
- speak softly
- plan your menus
- get to know your child's gifts and personality
- contentment, not comparison

SLOW SCHOOLING

- seek to have realistic expectations
- do not listen to or watch that which does not edify
- spend time laughing with your children
- a heavy dose of gratitude does wonders
- grow something
- sleep early, and sleep well
- relationship is more important than winning ribbons
- find grace in failure
- assure your children that they are wanted and needed
- keep learning
- teach good work habits to keep the home running
- expect interruptions and trials

EQUIPPING and CARING for the TEACHER

- let go of what is not working without guilt
- a little time outdoors every day
- expect to trip over toys, have to repaint, and repair books
- timeouts are not just for children
- make your bed and clean your sink every day
- it's all right to cry
- be honest about what is wasting your time, and cull
- ask for help
- you are not "called" to homeschool...you are "called" to faithfulness
- fellowship with the saints
- there's a difference between DOING and BEING

SLOW SCHOOLING

- less room for pride means more room for grace
- keep it simple
- mind the media
- service-oriented, not task-oriented
- there is no such thing as the perfect homeschool
- look for the lessons in every failure or trial
- above all, rest in the grace and love of Jesus

EQUIPPING and CARING for the TEACHER

BLOG

"Following After Patience"

Wednesday, October 3, 2007, 08:25am

I am not more patient than any other mother. I'm not. But if another woman looks at me in awe over the extraordinary patience she "sees" in me, I am not only going to thank the Lord for His reflection, I will use the opportunity to point her to the supply.

8

Teaching and Training

"It has been said that the essence of teaching is causing another to know. It may similarly be said that the essence of training is causing another to do. Teaching gives knowledge. Training gives skill. Teaching fills the mind. Training shapes the habits. Teaching brings to the child that which he did not have before. Training enables a child to make use of that which is already his

SLOW SCHOOLING

> possession. We teach a child the meaning of words. We train a child in speaking and walking. We teach him the truths which we have learned for ourselves. We train him in habits of study, that he may be able to learn other truths for himself."
>
> — H. Clay Trumbull

A proper parental perspective goes a long way in discipling a child. If children are a blessing as the psalms proclaim (specifically 127 and 128), then they are a blessing despite what the world and even our own vexed spirits believe, even in times of frustration or failure. If, on the other hand, they were simply add-ons to a full life, then surely we would find ourselves wanting to escape more, wanting to send them off and

TEACHING and TRAINING

away (even to "good schools" or the "best daycare" or to "great programs"). If my children are a blessing, then I need to choose to behave in that manner: I accept them, I love them, I desire them to be near (yea, even under my feet!), and I have an interest to train them so that they will in turn be a blessing to our nation and our world.

There is a plethora of helpful parenting books, and this is not going to address particular issues, mainly because I am certainly not a parenting expert! Furthermore, my oldest of nine is 26 years old; I still have a lot (a LOT) more parenting to do. In that sense, I am still much in the trenches with my mommy-peers. What I have experienced, however, is that home educating our children allows ample opportunities to witness and assess the growth, or lack of, good character. It also provides a

SLOW SCHOOLING

school of sorts to my own character growth, and therein lies the trouble of the matter. Desiring peace and quiet to fold laundry or even cook a small meal is not sinful, but demanding it leads to an exasperation that knows no bounds. Having children at home all day is as busy as, well, having children at home all day.

Slow schooling allows for children to engage in the everyday living of life, rather than setting apart a particular time or season to hit the books. Certainly there is a time to teach and a time to train, but teaching a child how to read is not the same thing as training a child to love reading. Obviously, modeling is a preferred means of training, and that is what discipling does: cultivates a desire and subsequently an ease in following the Master's (or mother's) footsteps.

TEACHING and TRAINING

As previously mentioned, slow schooling is not the same as unschooling. Slow schooling allows the parent to direct the child in academic studies deemed of importance, but with a flow that feels right in the season of life everyone is in. The goal in slow schooling is not necessarily the amount of literature read or how fast multiplication tables can be mastered, but in cultivating habits that will foster and bless lifelong learning.

For example, ignoring the climbing childhood chaos while trying to write an email or finish up a project means that poor habits of self-control and restraint are getting fed. Allowing for unmade beds (or whatever home cleanliness standards you may want to have) feeds habits of neglect and poor stewardship. The best time to gently steer the child to better habits is immediately, and immediately only

SLOW SCHOOLING

occurs Right Now. Otherwise, those little bugaboos end up as thistle seeds deeply implanted into hearts, and before you know it, character issues become downright prickly for anyone and everyone in contact with your child. Remember your "why" for home education. Would poor habits enable or dismantle those hopes and goals? Keeping your child at home with you means having the ability to meet those needs for correction, promptly.

Probably the greatest hindrance in slow schooling is the amount of time spent outside of the home. This is not only true for the child, no matter how wonderful the outside clubs or classes may be, but it is especially true for the homeschooling parents. Being at home physically is needful, but being present mentally and emotionally is also of grave

TEACHING and TRAINING

importance. Gadding about to other homes via social media or blogs or smartphones creates an environment where a child is more likely to recall seeing the back of Mama's head more than her sweet smile. It is a tragedy that even in public, parents are seen regularly engrossed in their smartphones at the expense of enjoying their child.

To train up your children in good habits, model those habits. If you desire them to be socially fit to be around people of all ages and stages and nationalities and personalities, then they must see you interacting with the same, with eye contact, smiles, and a genuine love. They will witness when and how you hug another or shake hands, and they will ponder your words when those people are away. They will know if you are sincere or hypocritical, acting one way, but speaking in another.

SLOW SCHOOLING

Socialization is a topic many people grabble with when discussing home education. Rest assured, if your child is involved in outside activities with other people, and they watch how you interact with people on a regular basis, they are not likely to be lonely or socially awkward. Rather, they will excel in loving their neighbors.

Say "yes" as much as possible. Playdough? Yes (though I'd rather not deal with making the table a mess). A piece of candy? Yes (it's been a while and I'd rather say "yes" than have them sneak one). Using scissors and glue and glitter? Um...yeeesssss (though I know it's going to take a long time to clean that up). Most times we say "no" because we dread the ramifications of what "yes" would mean, from muddy feet to scattered puzzle pieces. Let them be children and enjoy a childhood that tries a

TEACHING and TRAINING

variety of different things and experiences. That was part of your "why" to begin with, wasn't it? Cultivate curiosity and creativity, and they will carry that well into adulthood.

Teaching children to participate in running the household is also helpful in training good habits. That means taking the time to teach how to specifically do chores. They cannot leave home with the habits of clean laundry, washed dishes or a pleasant and healthy home without taking the time and effort to practice them. If you desire to raise up children who will delight in serving their spouses, children, church, neighbors, and nation, then practice, they must. Otherwise, they will expect to BE served. Training, like learning, happens at all times, and it is not always the lesson you hope for them to take to heart.

SLOW SCHOOLING

In training children to be lifelong learners, it helps for them to know you love them. This may seem obvious, but for some of us, simply smiling when a child comes into a room takes a little practice. Hugs, pats, kisses, sharing jokes and playing games, taking the time to listen to your son's new song (with beginner guitar enthusiasm), delighting in the crown of daisies your daughter wants to place upon your head—these are the kinds of occasions to daily delight in your child. Having a relaxed, smiling attitude will bear more fruit than any demanding and sour one, even while the parent is firm about expectations in both cases.

Lastly, let us not belittle the habit of simply being present around family members, fellow sinners. Are certain children more difficult than others? Are there personality conflicts? How about arguments, or differences in opinions or

TEACHING and TRAINING

tastes? Emotional roller-coasters, special needs, and struggles for privacy? Health needs and outside trials? Well, how will they ever learn how to function in the Real World if they do not practice in the safety and under the loving guidance of people in their own home? How will they learn that, while we were yet sinners, Christ died for us? Or where will they practice forgiveness, seventy times seven times?

Slow schooling is not simply about learning how to read on a child's own timing; it is about training lifelong habits with an eternal perspective in mind. Yes, it involves a homeschooling parent's full attention and heart. Yes, it means making sacrifices. But can you think of anything more precious than your child's value and potential in bringing glory to God?

SLOW SCHOOLING

BLOG

"Education of a Sheeple"

Wednesday, April 30, 2007, 04:03pm

Many people I know roll their eyes when I suggest bringing their children home as a means of restoring and repairing their families because I simply don't know the issues involved with their children. The parent claims she doesn't have the patience. Or there isn't time. Or it's just "not for them". Or their kids deserve the "best" ("best" being judged by the amount of money it takes). Or it is too hard. Or that it's a hopeless proposition. So, it goes. "Just wait" they tell me about my own children, "until they're ten (or teenagers....)" They insist upon pressing their

TEACHING and TRAINING

children onwards to the *best* of everything, college accounts readied before teeth were cut. I say, let us see. Let us wait, slow to make assumptions and expectations of their lives. Let us instead be one in heart, in relationship, in the peace and joy of the Lord. Let us see where your talents and skills lead. And let us see what He will do....

9

TODDLERS TO BIG KIDS

BLOG

"Homeschooling a Toddler"

Tuesday, November 13, 2007, 09:23am

> Sometimes I have to wonder at how hard we make it in teaching our toddlers.... I never stressed about how to teach any of my toddlers how to walk as babies and I didn't buy curriculum to teach them to form words. But, somehow, they turn three or four and PANIC

SLOW SCHOOLING

sets in. What if I don't teach them right? What if I miss the key hour for implanting the understanding of the numeric system? What if, what if...they don't get into a private college on a full scholarship ride on their way to making $300,000 a year all because I didn't have (gasp!) the right manipulatives to stretch their brains?!

I love toddlers. I love their chubby little hands, their moist pursed kissie lips, and their wide wondering eyes. I love how, when finding out there is a boundary, they smile up at you while pointing their little feet *just* over the line to see if anything happens. And they're so busy! One minute they're in your cupboards taking out all

TODDLERS to BIG KIDS

of the pans, and the next they are in your refrigerator taking out all of the fruit. Toddlerhood is a real time of training in what the routines and rules of the household are, and what the consequences of breaking them might be. Many, if not most, issues with disobedience and attitude can be addressed during this age. However, adults are fairly distracted and seem to either tend towards moralism or child-centered parenting, or expect that their children will get with the program on their own or with a touch of behavioral modification.

It is small wonder, therefore, that most of them are rushed through potty training, packed up and sent away to go to preschool, regardless of the harm in social and emotional development that may occur.[1] By the time they reach the stage of leveling the house with the energy of a Tazmanian devil, both the homemaking mother and the family dog are ready for a respite. Families most concerned with keeping their children home will work diligently to address issues of character—both their child's and their own—recognizing that it is God's grace that enables them to persevere as needed. There are many books that Christian parents have been blessed with, both addressing the necessary perspective and providing procedures in child training.[2] If parenting has become chaotic, I would encourage the reader to persistent study and prayer in overcoming the challenge(s), rather than simply sending the small child away for another adult to address the issues. Seek wisdom from other (successful!) parents who have children you enjoy having around.

In our home, toddlers are most successful if they know they are not only loved, but that

TODDLERS to BIG KIDS

they are wanted and needed. They help with the cooking, the cleaning, and wiping the baby's hands. They go to the market with me, fold the washcloths, and learn how to make their own beds. In every day, they are incorporated into the workings of running a home and growing a garden. The easiest way to grow a teenager who is annoyed with chores is to wait until the child is a teenager to expect them to work. Certainly there are times when toddlers seem underfoot, but that time is short and the lessons learned long. Toddlers will know they belong if they have important work to do, for the good of the family.

Routines are key in helping a toddler to thrive. Meal times, naptimes, and bedtimes ought to be at regular times; when those are mastered, it is easier to add in other parts of the day, such as table time or play time (more on

SLOW SCHOOLING

those to come). Practically speaking, those kinds of strict routines require us to stay home except for our once-a-week outing. As another benefit to regular routines and meal time, cleaner diets are easier to prepare and serve, giving the toddler additional support for good physical, mental and emotional health, attitudes, and actions.

Lastly, careful commands and a relaxed, smiling attitude does much to win the day. By careful commands, I mean not asking the child to do something you are not in a position to follow up with in case of disobedience. If you are currently snaking out a toilet clog, it probably isn't the best time to ask your toddler to go pick up her crayons. But if you choose to do so, keep that relaxed smiling attitude if you need to immediately drop what you're doing in order to help her do what you've asked.

TODDLERS to BIG KIDS

Below (and the pages that follow) are activities and supplies our family has used in homeschooling our toddlers and small children. Some, such as reading aloud or chores, are daily occurrences. These are children that need constant attention and supervision and continual inspection for chores and jobs to be well done. They are still in training, and the main goal of these years is to capture their hearts for Jesus Christ, that the rest of their years will be an outworking of character development by grace through the working of the Holy Spirit.

- chores (home economics and life skills, personal and clothing care, etc.)
- reading aloud
- practicing instruments

SLOW SCHOOLING

- Bible memory work (we like Scripture Memory Fellowship for that)
- playing outdoors
- learning full name, address, and phone number
- Lauri puzzles and toys (they will replace missing parts!)
- floor puzzles
- music lessons
- phonics games
- lacing
- jump ropes and rebounders
- bingo
- sand writing/box
- tracing and printing his or her name
- stamping

TODDLERS to BIG KIDS

- coloring (try other crayons such as beeswax, too)
- make place cards for the table
- building blocks
- construction toys
- number drills (hop 5 times, clap 8 times, etc.)
- clay
- finger painting
- inside tents, outside tents
- scissors & glue
- seesaws, swings
- math and science manipulatives
- drawing
- giant Tonka trucks and mini Matchbox cars
- beanbags and targets

SLOW SCHOOLING

- go outside
- watercolors
- stickers
- nature walks
- listening and drawing to classical music (what does it make you think of?)
- earning money through chores
- using a field guide for birds and plants
- measuring everything (how long is our table, how high is your bed...)
- sorting (beans, buttons, coins, washers, keys, M&M's, animal crackers...)
- matching games
- magazine collage
- write the grandparents

TODDLERS to BIG KIDS

- oral narration (tell me all about the book we read)
- crafts
- toy boats
- dress-up play
- books on tape (the best ones are the ones Mommy or Daddy record!)
- call Grandma or Grandpa
- counting backwards
- use dice to roll and then count jumps, blocks, toys to pick up, etc.
- Lego or Duplo
- stencils
- rubber stamps
- playdough
- illustrate poems read aloud

SLOW SCHOOLING

- board games (Chutes and Ladders, anyone?)
- educational computer games
- buttons (be wary of a choking hazard)
- baking measurements (cups, ounces, etc.)
- bubble pipes
- telling time
- making pictures for grandparents
- magnets
- outdoor sand boxes
- stringing large beads
- pegboards
- making placemats
- using a calendar
- watercolors

TODDLERS to BIG KIDS

- garden tools sized for little hands
- puppets
- card games (Memory, etc.)
- tricycles, scooters
- crafts and handwork (toddlers in other parts of the world spin and knit!)
- making bookmarks
- field trips to the farm, beach, post office (behind the scenes), etc.
- sorting (buttons, beans, seeds, beads...use a muffin tin)
- water play
- kites and pinwheels
- markers (washable!)
- flannel and felt boards
- counting money

SLOW SCHOOLING

- visit the library (often)
- miniature people and animals (Playmobile for example)
- have I mentioned the great outdoors yet?
- picking flowers
- seed pictures/mosaics
- yarn pictures
- hammering nails
- workbooks from Rod and Staff (preschool) or other companies
- sidewalk chalk
- soccer balls, whiffle balls, tennis balls...
- planting seeds
- making or playing instruments
- reading books

TODDLERS to BIG KIDS

- writing in a journal
- helping in the kitchen (or laundry or bedroom....)
- fingerplays

Lastly, I recommend Ruth Beechick's books;[3] her ideas make homeschooling effective and fun, and they can release you from the pressure of making your home into a school. Have the wet washcloths ready, and let the finger painting commence! No aspirin, school buses, or tuition necessary.

Here is an example from a day in teaching my children when they were all small:

SLOW SCHOOLING

BLOG

"Teaching Small Children"

Wednesday, February 27, 2008, 10:53am

My preschool/kindergarten time for my 3 and 6-year-old begins around 9am. Where is everyone else?

The 7-year-old is doing his music practice and watching the baby. The 10-year-old is doing her morning chores and music practice. The baby (21-month-old) is playing alone in his playpen (in full view of older brother) for 30 minutes, and then plays with his brother once music practice is complete. I have found that breaking up my children into smaller groups of two at the table make it easier for me to focus.

TODDLERS to BIG KIDS

The first thing that happens with my two "students" is some Bible study. For my 3-year-old, it looks like coloring a page from a story we've just learned or read.

"For my 6-year-old, she is working on her Bible notebook. She is copying a verse I gave to her, illustrating it, and then completing the statement, "This means...."

I like that they can self-start on something independently, because it gives me a moment to gather my thoughts and any supplies I might need while they work.

After about 5 minutes or so (depending on how engrossed she may or may not be that day), I

SLOW SCHOOLING

begin working with the 3-year-old. This day, we worked on cutting and pasting figures with numbers on them (in order). Then, because she is a very busy and "hands on" girl, we got out the buttons and counted the right amount for each figure (one button on the "1", two on the "2" and so forth). She started to wane when we got to five, so we put that away.

I thought she should do a Lauri puzzle, but she still had her hands into the buttons, digging and looking at all the colors. So we brought out some color cards and began putting red buttons on the red card, and so on.

By this time, 30 minutes had passed and it was time for her to

TODDLERS to BIG KIDS

clean up and go play with her big sister. Other things we do during this time might be working out of workbooks, playing with letter stencils, stringing beads, doing puzzles, or easy, artsy crafts. We love the Rod and Staff workbooks; they are easy to do, and thankfully inexpensive. She is read to a lot during the day as well (along with her siblings!).

Meanwhile, my 6-year-old is working on her math...or her spelling....

Every day she does work with reading and phonics with writing in her journal, Spelling Power, Reading Made Easy or Explode the Code (never all in the same day!). She always does work in math as

SLOW SCHOOLING

well. Sometimes that is from a workbook, other times it is completely hands on.

When my 6-year-old is finished with those tasks, she gets to work on what she really likes to do: a craft. Currently, she is working on her collage castle, an activity we got from Usborne's *Things to Make and Do With Paper*.

Sometimes the two of them will do a task from the book, *Making the Most of the Preschool Years*. By 10:00 (an hour later) we are all packed up and heading down for "Bible Time" with everyone else. After that is snack time, and time for the older two to get to work while these two girls go off to play (the baby eats his snack and either naps in his bed or plays in his playpen—depending on his mood!).

You know, no teacher will love on your babies and care about how they are doing more than you, and that is reason enough to keep them home even without all of the "research." Enjoy teaching and being with your small children; they are only little once!

BLOG
"Preschool at Home"
Wednesday, February 27, 2008, 10:04am

I am so thankful to have my children at home, every one of them. I am grateful not to miss

SLOW SCHOOLING

out on the funny things they say and the opportunities to quickly correct them when they do something wrong. I love the amazing front row seat I have to watch their ever-expanding minds grow, learn and stretch. I know when to challenge them in their schoolwork, and when to back off. And while I do not pressure them to keep up with anyone else, I can lovingly push them to achieve their potential. I am here to provide nutritious snacks when they're hungry, and bandaids and hugs when they're bleeding from bicycle boo-boos. I love learning alongside with them, digging into ancient history or impressionist artists, and nothing beats the ongoing banter that occurs during chore time or meals.... Homeschooling

TODDLERS to BIG KIDS

a preschooler is as easy as putting him or her onto your lap for a good story.

10

Middles Through the Teen Years

BLOG

"Mental Gymnastics"

Tuesday, August 19, 2007, 04:31pm

> I'm trying to figure out the *perfect* time to begin a full schedule of homeschooling again, with the *perfect* mix of curriculum.
>
> ...hahahahahahhahahahahahaha....

SLOW SCHOOLING

Slow schooling through the middle and high school ages can be some of the best years as a homeschooling parent. After spending the early years working diligently to teach basic reading, writing and arithmetic (and gleaning from many, many other subjects during the pursuit of said "three R's"), the older children are in a position to not only begin to self-direct their own learning, but to own it for life.

The middle years, around 12-14 years, are what I consider the "passing the baton" years. These are the years we begin to earnestly consider what interests and inherit talents our children have, and to think about steering them toward their strengths. Some children are naturally more oriented towards the language arts and are eager readers or writers; others would rather work equations or figure out how things work. Other children prefer to spend their

MIDDLES THROUGH the TEEN YEARS

time in the arts, constantly crafting in something or another, while others are outdoors most of the time, turning over rocks if they are not already climbing them. You'll begin to get a good sense of how they work and relate with others, and what motivates them.

During these years, I teach my children to keep a planner. A planner can be as simple as a daily piece of scrap paper. At the beginning of the day, we go over what needs to be done that day, and write a list: math assignments, feeding the animals, even "up-n-ready" if they still have not mastered the basics of morning preparation, such as making their bed. I might ask them about any projects they are working on and write those down as well. Because we have regular routines in our home, they know exactly when they will have the time to work on them.

SLOW SCHOOLING

At these ages, I am still doing quite a bit of the teaching. One child may need extra help with spelling, another using new math tools. But my job as a homeschooler has become less as a teacher, and more as a manager. I manage which curriculum fits each child best, which extracurricular activity fits the best, and of course the time in which they have to accomplish these things. We work on time management, and then on persistence when events or circumstances threaten to derail our efforts. I work harder on character issues because I want them to become self-directed learners. I move them as quickly as possible from the conformist and entitlement mindset of "tell me what to do" to shifting them towards ambition, responsibility, and having the willingness to take risks. They have heard me say often, especially when dealing with poor attitudes or faulty self-debasements, that "It is MY job to

MIDDLES THROUGH the TEEN YEARS

provide you with an education, but it is YOUR job to learn." The middle years are a time of letting the children have more responsibilities with greater freedoms, but also a time of reigning them back in for more one-on-one teaching as needed.

One idea to help your child to own their education is to be an enthusiastic supporter of whatever they think they may want to do. If they want to be chicken farmers, then get them a dozen books from the library all about chicken breeds and, if you are able, let them raise a bunch of poultry. Work with them to start a small egg business and never ever tell them that chicken farming is unrealistic, stupid, or too much hard work. If your child grows up to happily raise up poultry and provide amazingly healthy eggs to his community at large while staying out of debt and enjoying his lifestyle, why would that be so bad?

The truth is that their interests may come and go, or one thing in particular will stick. Don't get so invested in your own dream of what your children will or won't do for a living that you stifle their own decision-making abilities. Some of the best, most high-achieving people in our culture never even finished school. But they learned to set goals and overcome barriers, and that is something that is not necessarily taught through a textbook.

Let me give you an example from my then 11-year-old daughter. I already knew she had a bent towards thoughtful, diligent, and excellent work, and she also seemed to excel and enjoy math and science. One day, I asked her what she thought she might be interested in doing,

MIDDLES THROUGH the TEEN YEARS

and she mentioned two things: raising hens (yes, that was my daughter), and working for NASA. So while we were able, she raised many, many hens (all with individual names of course). But we also went online and looked into what the requirements were for working at NASA. We discovered that there were several degrees that would be acceptable, such as one in mathematics. We decided that if NASA was the goal, then she would need to study higher math, and we planned that out. We also arranged for her to meet Richard Gordon, a retired NASA astronaut, when he visited our community, and she shook his hand in the hallway telling him about her ambition.

I don't think NASA is still on her radar, but it made for an easy answer to give her on those mornings when she asked if she HAD to do her assignments: "Well, you don't have to, but that's

SLOW SCHOOLING

what it takes to get to NASA...." Once you connect the dots from the work at hand to the work they dream of, your job of motivating, bribing, or begging your student is finished. Their purpose isn't focused on pleasing you or making a letter grade, but on doing the life work they feel inspired, called, and enthusiastic about pursuing.

This is the point at which we have mostly parent-recommended, but child self-directed, learning. If a homeschooling parent has been patient with educating their younger child, taking into account maturity levels, and if that parent has put more focus into character building than completing a particular curriculum (though character CAN be built through bringing something to completion), then it is likely that the parent will still wield a

MIDDLES THROUGH the TEEN YEARS

great amount of influence over their child's education.

There is a cost, however, in customizing an education in this way. Conformity and obedience to social and cultural mandates is not only expected, but rewarded. If your child desires an education that does not follow the current methodology, be prepared for funny looks at best.

In the rest of the book, we'll look at specific areas of education, including life and work training, and why we as parents still need to keep our hands to the plow to direct the education and training up of our children, even as we allow those very unique arrows to ultimately direct where they will go.

11

Life Skills

BLOG

"Pressing On..."

Monday, April 23, 2007, 02:45pm

My 7yo son has put together and fastened a battery-powered cable car that runs from the dining room window to the upstairs railing. I imagine at 17 he will be doing the same thing, only from a 50 foot high tree house to the ground, for the purpose of bringing up his dog. Would that count on a high school transcript?

Most children are run through the public system as if he or she is college-bound to inevitably work a lifetime for a corporation. That system fails the children that are more gifted or eager to work with their hands in a trade, create in the arts, or coax food from the ground. Because our society thrives when people fulfill their own innate talents and bents for the good of others, it doesn't make the education a future CEO needs inherently worth more than the training for rug weaving. And making more money isn't the best indicator of happiness, which is, most parents say, what they want more than anything else for their children: to be happy.

LIFE SKILLS

Historically, children of all ages were taught in a trade or how to do handwork in order to further the family economy, and as a result, further the economies of their communities. Children as young as four were taught to spin and knit,[1] and as young as six were expected to have at least a working knowledge of the flora and fauna growing naturally around their homes.[2] This training was not at the expense of receiving a decent education. Regardless of the current relevancy of the infamous "eighth grade examinations,"[3, for example] it is clearly seen that even the tradesmen and farmers were not dimwits.

Regardless of what life work our children will undertake, they will still need to take care of the basics of survival: food, clothing, and shelter. In our day, this may be translated as: knowing how to procure and cook food,

SLOW SCHOOLING

knowing how to wash and dry clothing, and knowing how to keep a home that is safe, clean, and healthy. The most logical way to teach children these skills is to ensure that they are needed, working members of the household, each with their own responsibilities and chores. A toddler may begin with how to make her bed in the morning; a teenager ought to know how to keep the entire house, including how to turn on and off the electricity, water, and gas. These are simply the basics—how to get by—not what someone would need to truly thrive.

There are many resources available if a parent needs help with regards to what chores might be appropriate for any particular age (see the Maxwell's work, for example[4]). The biggest challenge is not in coaxing children to work; it is in allowing them to make mistakes, make messes, and take four times longer than

LIFE SKILLS

an adult to do the same task. Unfortunately, the more a parent pushes aside a child to "go play" while the important work is tended to, the more that child will rebel later when pleaded with to help around the house and yard. It is not loving to do everything for them; it is setting them up to be resentful or angry when others cannot or do not cater to their wants (which inevitably turn into needs), and sowing slothfulness into their hearts. Teach them to wash a dish today, and they won't wait for someone else to do it tomorrow.

Another side benefit in working chores is that many of them, especially at the onset, require explanation, observation, and trial and error. This may sound like a burden to the parent who may rightly desire a little peace and quiet, but it plants by faith the fruit of a close, loving relationship as time is spent together talking and walking by the way. How else will your child learn to think your thoughts after you, or appreciate how and why you do things the way that you do? How might they honor your heritage if you never chat about what your own grandparents were like, or know the customs and manners of your family or faith? To expect a child that is often away from the parent to suddenly appreciate and embrace that parent's values is unrealistic and unreasonable.

That's not to say I've taught every child of mine to do every chore. As my children grew, they also took on the responsibilities to teach their siblings. I appreciate the opportunity to have them work (and bond) together, especially as it is most likely that they will outlive their father and I. We desire for them all to be close. What better way to encourage

LIFE SKILLS

that than to put them to work to clean the van or the duck pen together?

Here is an example of chores that my children did when they were younger, as written on my first blog:

BLOG
"Blessing Ahead: Children At Work"
Wednesday, October 10, 2007, 08:23am

All my children are expected to be "up and ready" before breakfast. This means: dressed, face washed, teeth and hair brushed, pjs away and beds made. I wish this happened every day, but we work on it as a goal (if you never have a target, how are you ever going to hit it?). In addition to their "up and ready" chores, these are some

SLOW SCHOOLING

of the jobs my children regularly do around the house:

9yo

- feeds and cares for the animals
- teaches and trains the toddler
- launders girls sheets and remakes the beds
- launders and replaces towels
- launders the girls clothing
- bakes all sorts of breads and desserts
- vacuums and mops
- loads dishwasher
- weeds

7yo

- helps with animal care

LIFE SKILLS

- cleans out the cat litter box
- launders the boys clothing
- sweeps and mops
- empties all garbage cans
- washes garbage cans
- clears the table
- launders boys sheets and remakes beds
- weeds
- cleans out the garage

5yo

- feeds the cat
- sweeps kitchen floor
- empties the dishwasher
- folds and puts away towels
- dusts
- cleans windows

SLOW SCHOOLING

- cleans out the van
- straightens up our library
- sets the table

3yo

- sweeps the floor
- T.P. runabout
- puts silverware away
- folds and puts away napkins
- dusts
- straightens the mud room
- puts away dirty towels and napkins
- puts away clean diapers from the dryer
- helps set the table

Also, they all have an assigned area to keep clean (in addition to

LIFE SKILLS

their room). My 7-year-old is in charge of the hallway and upstairs bathrooms, my 5-year-old is in charge of the playroom and loft, and my 9-year-old is in charge of the downstairs. Separating their own "zones" was very helpful because it became OBVIOUS who was and who wasn't doing their jobs!

The oldest three are at times "in charge" of their 3-year-old sister, and usually she will just tag along and "help" whomever with whatever job is going on. This is great on a number of fronts: both siblings bond, one learns to teach, the other gets to learn a new skill. This is my "ducks in a row" picture: I'm the Mama duck, and teach the eldest, who teaches the next one, who teaches the next

SLOW SCHOOLING

one.... What this frees me up to do is oversee each one individually and give them each attention as they need and want it. I do not have to run around "doing everything." This means I do not have to burn out and play the martyr, and that my children are not robbed of the opportunity to gain life skills, foster good relationships, and grow in responsibility. Yes, it would be "easier" to ship them all away from my home so that I could scrub a toilet in peace...but sparkling toilets pale in comparison to time spent learning and growing together as a family.

LIFE SKILLS

The family has been hard pressed since the Industrial Revolution to work together as a family in the pursuit of economic gain and financial freedom. Once fathers left the home to find work, women and children were left on their own to keep the home and, in many instances, the land. The home slowly became a place where living became separated from production—that is, it became a place where things were consumed, not produced. It seems to me that a woman, between missing the companionship and vision of her husband, and the seemingly mundane stoking the home fires without gaining any sense of community purpose, would have been provoked to a discontent and stress that otherwise would have been abated with the family unit left whole.

Thus, once it became understandable, even fashionable, for a woman to leave the home in order to find outside employment with which to add to the family economy, there was nothing of purpose for children to do within the home setting. Sunday schools were implemented to rescue these wayward children, to provide for them a safe environment and an education that might equip them to be upstanding citizens and good workers for their own future families. It didn't take long for the government to take this model and create the public school system we have today.

With homes empty now for three quarters of the day, is it any wonder that family relationships are strained? With every member about the business of doing individual work, there isn't much other than love to bond the family. And when love becomes difficult—as it inevitably does between sinners—there isn't

LIFE SKILLS

anything else to keep the family together through the worst of times.

One of the blessings of slow schooling is the momentum that it can stimulate when a family gets a vision for developing a home business. With at least one parent at home, and a different view of education and preparation for life, the family can begin to contemplate and even execute means to bring income into the home. Even for our youngest and most inexperienced, our current day is ripe with opportunity for education and the means to produce, for a global market. Furthermore, the Industrial model is fading away before our very eyes as we are not on the cusp but rather at the base of the hockey stick curve of a technological revolution that will profoundly change how goods are produced and delivered. There is a great and as yet untapped wealth of favorable circumstances that can give a family the freedom to work together to create the lifestyle they want and enjoy.

Perhaps this sounds improbable, impossible even. Consider, however, the probable fact that you may not have seen a family practice in this way because you grew up within the last hundred years. If we were to expand our view a bit to the thousands upon thousands of years previous, you might see the very normal practice of closely bonded families living and working together, with businesses based out of their homes. It is not that this is a new and different idea; it is the original idea that has been distorted in the pursuit to create a more materialistic and consumer-based lifestyle.

There are many ways to oil the gears in considering how a family might produce goods

LIFE SKILLS

together. A very effective way is to consider what the innate talents and interests of the parents might be. Does Dad have an appreciation for woodworking, engraving, or working with textiles? Does Mom have an eye for design, a ready pen to write with, a green thumb? Many times a parent may remember the great pleasure they derived with certain hobbies as a youth, but feel that those things were put away along with other childish things. I'd like to encourage you to take those "childish things" out of the attic boxes!

Perhaps a father enjoyed martial arts as a young lad. Could he take a few years to get training and then begin to offer his own classes? Or it may be that a mother was quite skilled in sewing aprons and pillows in her middle school economics class. Could she take an internet webinar to learn how to market and sell them?

SLOW SCHOOLING

In this way, a family could offer training in life skills or produce goods for use, but it gets even better: once these are firmly grasped, a family can take these models and use them to produce passive income.

Passive income is the income a family earns while they are sleeping. The father that is teaching martial arts might put together an ebook of the best practices to become a better martial artist—one that blows away the "Top three tips" someone might find on the internet search engine. The mother sewing aprons might put together a video series that would teach even the youngest novice to sew with skill. These products, once produced, have the potential to reach millions, and because they are products ONCE produced do not need any more work in order to continue to bring in income. In this way, the family not only takes

LIFE SKILLS

advantage of the massive education available that others have put together, they add to the growing body of knowledge for the worldwide community.

Not sure where to start? Your childhood talents and interests don't pique your interest anymore? Then dig around your children's talents and interests a bit—what excites them? If the only thing that is floating their boats right now is getting the next high score on a video game, then a media fast might break through the fog of hallucination to encourage more edifying and valuable pursuits (this is true for Dad and Mom, too!).

A valuable resource for us has been the Keepers of the Faith club.[5] They have unfortunately closed, but their handbooks were helpful in choosing a wide variety of activities

SLOW SCHOOLING

for our family to try. Things that my husband and I have learned with our children (not having had any prior childhood experience) are: gardening, animal husbandry—including milking and butchering—baking bread and making butter, woodworking, basket weaving, handwork such as knitting and crochet, food preservation, website design and internet marketing, soap making and electrical work. If you can't find a Keepers of the Faith handbook, you may be able to find an old Girl Scout or Boy Scout book in a used bookstore. Those little handbooks are a treasure trove of "What could we do next? What sounds interesting?"

Many people are concerned about the self-esteem and confidence of our young people. The way to produce bold and hopeful people is not to lie to them about the world being their oyster, and how they can be or do "anything."

LIFE SKILLS

Rather, it is to give them time and space to think deeply, allow them a little boredom to cultivate an imagination, and encourage and expect them to work hard. We can also provide for them the opportunity to develop life skills and show them how, even as adults, there is no excuse not to keep learning something. Confidence arises not only from having a right understanding of self ("I'm not the most important person on the planet"), but from having the ability and willingness to serve their family, and then their community, with enthusiasm for having done a thing well, whatever that may be. Give them the chance and the freedom to do so.

SLOW SCHOOLING

BLOG

"Keepers of the Faith Club"
Sunday, September 9, 2007, 05:29pm

What I love most about Keepers is that our children are learning real life skills, and these in turn develop their confidence. When they are turned loose to the world, they will have more important matters to consider than to spend time mentally spinning on how to work a washing machine. Teaching them these skills now buys them freedom from confusion and frustration later, and I enjoy using Keepers rewards and materials to that end.

12

Experiences

BLOG

"Civil War as a Family Affair"
Monday, June 26, 2006, 02:20pm

> We...met a family who worked together to run their own lunch business: Mom and Dad cooked, the 5-year-old took and gave orders, and the 3-year-old took care of the register as Mom looked on....

SLOW SCHOOLING

It goes without saying that a child's life is more than "preparing for life." The child IS living here and now! Certainly there are times in which to focus on learning new skills for future goals (such as learning letter sounds to encourage reading), but there also ought to be plenty of times simply to play or to create projects or even to "waste time." After all, those experiences unquestionably add to growth of brain, character, and stature as well.

The most basic experience that a child needs is to grow up in a stable, safe, and loving family. Unfortunately that foundation, when faulty, is frequently a cause of stress in even the smallest child and hinders his or her development. The best "experience" you can offer your child in terms of growing to adulthood is an everyday environment where

EXPERIENCES

both parents are committed to one another, for better and for worse.

As homeschoolers, time is much more fluid and frees you to pursue interests and to undertake new activities or hobbies. One of the best ways to stir the pot, so to speak, is to peruse the nonfiction stacks at the library. What subjects put the glimmer in your child's eye? Pile up the books, take them home, and see if an enthusiasm stirs up. From there, it is relatively easy to find educational videos or courses online, but make sure to balance the screen time with actual real-life experiences, with real people and/or the real outdoors.

There are many educational opportunities within most communities. Many towns have a community center with a plethora of classes offered, everything from foreign languages to gymnastics to photoshop to making homemade brooms. One of the most well-known and respected community resources is 4H, an organization that teaches children through hands-on projects in areas like health, science, agriculture and citizenship. Children not only learn the field they are in (such as rabbitry, robotics, or archery), but leadership skills and recordkeeping, too. Meeting times, fees, and requirements vary by club.[1]

There are also many events nearby that a child could have the chance to participate in, such as auditioning and participating in a theater show, volunteering for a neighborhood cleanup, or attending master gardening meetings. Naturally, groups may have reasonable age requirements, but most are met with the companionship of a parent. It is simply another way that a child or a parent may

EXPERIENCES

dabble in the interests of the other and make good memories together.

A child that has a specific interest may find an opportunity for shadowing, or apprenticing, with someone in that particular field. As examples, my daughter worked many years and learned to sew alongside a tailor who designed and sewed costumes for a renowned theater in Seattle. My son shadowed his father in the use of audio and sound equipment and learned how to control the mixer boards. If your child has a specific interest in, say, marine biology, is it possible to find a respected person in the business who wouldn't mind a shadow for a specified amount of time?

History buffs might find reenactments their cup of tea, and many of these groups travel across the nation, setting up camps and

SLOW SCHOOLING

reenacting battle scenes. They become fully immersed in the experience, much like learning a foreign language in another country.[2]

Speaking of visiting other countries, homeschooling allows for the flexibility to travel at any time in the year. Many churches offer short mission or ministry work in other countries. My hope regarding these trips is that they are used not *only* to build a house or two, but to clearly preach and present the gospel. Missionary trips also seem to bear more fruit when an ample amount of time is invested into the community: years, not weeks. Absent preaching the gospel, perhaps we ought to consider these trips as working vacations.

In any case, slow schooling offers an ample amount of freedom to fashion life experiences to fit the student and his or her family. There is no

EXPERIENCES

reason that education needs to be constrained to a book and pen.

13

Teaching the Bible

BLOG

"Bible Study for Children"

Tuesday, January 8, 2008, 12:45pm

The most needful thing I teach my children is how to read and study God's Word. There is so much promise of blessing for knowing and obeying God's voice, why on earth would I not want them to know how to read and understand the Bible for themselves? It is the most important time of our homeschool.

It wasn't so long ago that every literate person had a basic knowledge of the Bible. It didn't matter if you were a believer, an unbeliever, or a make-believer (hat tip to J. Vernon McGee), knowledge of the Bible was taught in the public schools and was foundational for a culture of common experience and good morals. Furthermore, this literary masterpiece was studied not only for the variety of genres, but for its history and scientific observations, and many would not know where phrases such as "the writing on the wall" came from, or even meant, without knowledge of the accounts within.

TEACHING the BIBLE

All of that is interesting but has no bearing on why we teach our children the Bible. We teach our children the Bible because it is the Word of God, and is "profitable for doctrine, for reproof, for correction, for instruction in righteousness" (2 Timothy 3:16). We desire our children to know and understand why their conscience rightly convicts them of wrongdoing, and to show them the law—the Ten Commandments—of which God has graciously made us all inherently aware. We want them to have an understanding of the whole arc of history, and to see how God's promises and prophecies were fulfilled in the coming of Jesus Christ. We want them to know the gospel, that Jesus did not die for the righteous, for those of no need, but for the broken and humble sinner, for a just and complete payment for the holy laws that had been—and would be—broken. And we have no greater joy than to see our children repent, trust Jesus, and walk in the light as He is the light, in truth.

It doesn't rightly matter how wonderful the education, how successful the career, how full the family or how happy the life is if a child loses his soul for eternity after the short vapor of a life he or she embraces. So we teach the Bible, praying always that sword of the Spirit will be quick and powerful.

The best way to do this is to simply read the Bible. We use the King James version as it is the easiest to understand, even for a child. We also use story books, and have listened to George Sarris read aloud beautifully on recording.

Below (and on the pages that follow) are several methods we have used throughout the years in our endeavor to teach the Bible. The

TEACHING the BIBLE

"method" is not as important as the consistent and persistent weight of importance you give not only on teaching the Bible, but on reading and studying it for yourself. Year by year, little by little, knowledge grows. We cannot save our own children—that is God's work—but we must be faithful to the task of teaching them diligently. If we truly love God, this will happen naturally.

- assign readings, either chapters or verses
- verse handwriting and copywork
- for toddlers, Christian coloring books
- memorization (we love Scripture Memory Fellowship for this)

SLOW SCHOOLING

- application: is there something in your reading that God wants you to know/do/be?
- read aloud: scripture, devotionals, story books, prayers
- read and sing the old hymns; they are rich in theology
- study the catechism
- learn how to use Bible study tools: atlas, dictionary, concordance
- teach how to do a topical or an inductive study
- faithful, local church attendance

TEACHING the BIBLE

- reports on people, places, events
- rewrite or retell accounts—drama, art, written assignments
- workbooks such as Studying God's Word
- *Proverbs* DVDs
- small group Bible studies
- vocabulary work, such as regeneration, sovereignty, propitiation
- Hebrew/Greek language study
- listen to orthodox preachers' sermons
- take a college level course

SLOW SCHOOLING

BLOG (continued)
"Bible Study for Children"
Tuesday, January 8, 2008, 12:45pm

We begin the school day with "Bible Time". What we do is gather around the couch, pray for understanding, and read a chapter out of a children's story or devotional book. We talk about what part both people played: the man (or woman) and God's. It's a good way to try to glean understanding, even for adults.

Then, we pray different prayers depending on what day it is: Monday— prayers of faith (needs/wants), Tuesday— prayers for family members, Wednesday— the

TEACHING the BIBLE

Lord's prayer, Thursday— prayers for missionaries/the persecuted, Friday— prayers for our church/pastor.

Afterwards, we work on our memory verses. We use books from Scripture Memory Fellowship and work towards prizes of other literature books and certificates.

For our individual Bible Study time... each child picks apart a Bible verse during the week. (I like to) use the *Doorposts For Instruction in Righteousness* to work with character issues as needed, and choose the verse for the week. These are their assignments during the week: Monday— write the verse, Tuesday— illustrate the verse, Wednesday—

SLOW SCHOOLING

write "This means...," Thursday—
write "I will...," Friday—
memorize verse and say it to
Daddy.

14

Teaching Writing

BLOG

"Happy Home Happenings"

Thursday, May 22, 2008, 11:20am

> Learning the three R's (and then some) continues. One thing I've changed is how I've approached teaching writing. After attending a workshop at the last conference and grilling a 12-year-old girl who participated in this program, I finally just bit the bullet (or

wallet) and bought the IEW program (Institute for Excellence in Writing). We've been at it a couple of weeks now and.....we LOVE it. Here is my 8-year-old "would rather play Lego than write" boy very intensely working on a three page paper.....and loving the process. Miracles do occur.

As a public school teacher, I was very much enamored with and enthusiastic about what was then known as the "Whole Language" movement. What was there not to be enthusiastic about? Surrounding—no, soaking—children in language at every turn, reading real (unabridged) books, and engaging them in the world of "writing workshops" where the written

TEACHING WRITING

word was encouraged, nurtured, and celebrated. I loved putting words all over the walls and introducing journal writing.

So it was with much gusto I embraced the same for my own children. And it was in following my own children through the years that the good and the bad made themselves to be really good, and really bad. The good: real literature and the love for writing. The bad: a real lack of modeling and poor mechanics. I understood the principle of using literature as a model, but other than an appreciation, my children did not know how to apply the same structure to write their own great works. Many times, it was something that ended up sounding forced, and furthermore, actually took away the joy of the reading when they knew they'd be encouraged (ie. "assigned") to write something halfway similar afterwards. Also, even though

SLOW SCHOOLING

a few of my children were very early readers (the youngest at four), spelling suffered despite multiple and very different attempts at correcting it. I began to wonder how my Whole Language students from my teaching years were faring as they progressed through the system. I wasn't comfortable with the idea "some people are bad spellers."

It was at a homeschool conference that I decided to listen in on a highly acclaimed writing curriculum. I was skeptical to say the least, but I had been humbled and was ready to try something new. Well. The lesson format made total sense and, for beginning writers, completely removed the strain of coming up with topics. The focus was on how to have solid structured writing, and with that incorporated timely lessons on mechanics. So we bit and took the program home. I watched the DVD's,

TEACHING WRITING

attempted the lessons myself, and put the Institute for Excellence in Writing (IEW) into practice. For our family, it was a hit for writing paragraphs and compositions. But it still didn't address the other problem: spelling.

Spelling seems to be one of those subjects that folks feel free to toss aside. The reason I usually hear is, "That's why we have spell check." Perhaps. Except that spell check is not only unreliable and potentially embarrassing, it misses the whole point of why we ought to have at least a base understanding of and respect for our English language.

For one, having a standardized means of spelling allows communication to be clear, not only today, but for future generations. Perhaps people purposely misspell their words (or ignore grammar rules, for that matter), but this is not reflective of God's own modeling and standard, to write "very plainly" (Deuteronomy 27:8). Writing "ur" for "you're" is not only lazy, but truly is disparaging the reader because that reader is going to have to work harder to try to understand the message you are attempting to communicate. And if you're not at least trying to be clear—or caring—then do not be surprised when your work is not treated with the respect you feel it deserves.

Secondly, spelling is not difficult. There are simply 70 basic phonograms in the English language, and 28 rules. Once those are mastered, the code is "cracked" and the exceptions are rare. For example, it becomes far easier to explain why c says /c/ in "cat" but says /s/ in ceiling. What makes spelling difficult, I believe, is in assuming children will learn how to spell simply by reading a lot.

TEACHING WRITING

Perhaps there are people that can and do, but I've met more than one "bad speller" who was an early reader. This, too, became a subject that I learned more about after I became a homeschooler than when I was a public school teacher getting paid to travel to other schools to teach other teachers how to teach Language Arts during their inservice days. But "phonics" was a curse word in the Whole Language world and flash cards for learning phonograms probably would not have been received well. *Spell to Write and Read* is the award-winning program we have used to train up our children in spelling, and it has been a blessing.

Teaching writing is very important—God sees the written word as important! Not only did He, Himself, write, but He commanded others to write, and keeps records.[1] And because He communicates very clearly, we, too,

SLOW SCHOOLING

ought to endeavor to communicate clearly. Communicating clearly not only means studying and applying standard English rules and spelling, but in careful and legible handwriting. There is much research regarding the importance of teaching cursive in brain development.[2, for example]

It goes without saying that children ought also to spend time in other writing endeavors: letter to relatives and pen pals, notes to everyone and for everything, journaling, thank you notes, assignments in other subjects. Like any other skill, it takes time, intent, and practice.

Teaching writing need not be difficult. This is one subject that I was supposedly an "expert" on but still saw a great need for improvement and am thankful that I found excellent training

TEACHING WRITING

to become a better teacher. However, I was also very, very motivated because I happen to *love* writing and the English language. Math and Science? Not so much, even though I recognize the great importance in studying God's orderly world. In the next chapters I will share with you other means of equipping your child in whatever subject you need help with.

15

Teaching Reading

BLOG

"Of Spitballs and Speedbumps"

Monday, June 18, 2007, 09:52am

I should have known better. But once my children found my stash of Calvin and Hobbes books, they were hooked. Suddenly anything else worth reading was buried under blankets, clothing and toys, and I was sure to regularly find grubby little hands clutching collections

SLOW SCHOOLING

of stories of this little boy with his stuffed toy tiger. Soon I was fielding questions such as, "Mom, what's a spitball?" and trying to join in on the laughter about Calvin creating speed bumps all over the grassy lawn (all the while I'm giving the "don't you dare" look).

My five-year-old graduated directly from easy phonic books and plunged into spending copious amounts of time giggling through the exploits of these characters.... It just goes to show you that while boxes of expensive phonic and reading programs may make you feel better about giving your child a "good education," it won't give them the same motivation to read as the

TEACHING READING

```
opportunity to learn about storing
snowballs in coat pockets, locking
babysitters out of the house, and
creating volcanoes out of mashed
potatoes.
```

In one sense, reading happens. Given enough opportunity, modeling, motivation and coaching, reading is a skill that most children can master. And, like walking, it doesn't matter much if the skill was mastered early on or later in childhood. Both early and late readers alike can learn to read well and read deeply. The challenge is that there is too much noise competing for reading time, and it isn't so much the ability to read that is at stake, but the willingness to read. There is a vast difference between people who are functionally illiterate

SLOW SCHOOLING

and those who are voluntarily so. It's important for our children to choose to read.

Why?

Given that God so clearly commanded His Word to be written, it follows that people could be expected to read and clearly understand it. The very foundation for the sanctity of every life and for individual liberty rests plainly upon an understanding of the nature of God and man. Truly, the only way to enslave another person is to keep that person illiterate, for he will be without knowledge and utterly dependent. Furthermore, whether or not he listens to his conscience, he is expected to be obedient to the laws of God and will perish if he persists in breaking them without restitution in Christ. How can he heed God without knowing how to read the Bible? He will be a reed

TEACHING READING

blowing wherever and however the cultural and fleshly wind blows.

As a homeschooling mother, my attitude was (and is) thus: there was great emphasis in teaching my child to read. It was (and is) a great blessing when that skill is attained, for their education is now more powerfully within their own hands, and they can read for themselves God's Word.

At the start is an environment of literacy. Thankfully, the library is free, and oh, how lovely the smell of fraying old chapter books and the sounds of rustling paper. It's a wonderful place to sample and carry home piles of books and yet maintain food money. We regularly have 50 or more library books in our home. Sadly, however, it is at times sorry not to find quality Christian classics among the stacks.

SLOW SCHOOLING

Therefore, I think it most needful in creating that environment of literacy to maintain a fair library in the home.

Reading aloud is golden from the infant on the knee to the teen at the table. It is not something to be done too quickly, or with a droning tone. The reader must enter the text, boom the voice when it's exciting and whisper when it's still and sad. Reading aloud is a time of gathering together to experience and learn with one another; it ought to be a time to look forward to. Don't discount reading aloud in the family home. After all, it was a read aloud that led to great repentance in Nehemiah 8! Read aloud proverbs, newspaper articles, poems, storybooks and unabridged novels. Read aloud advertisements and pick them apart for marketing ploys. And, of course, read aloud the

TEACHING READING

children's own writing and work, and teach them how to read aloud, too.

More often, reading aloud happens in spurts. Daddy might read a devotional before bed. I will try to get in a reading at lunch (having eaten ahead of time). "Read aloud" time might be counted with audiobooks as we travel, or when a child reads *Piggy and Gerald* for the 314th time to a younger sibling. It is never perfect in our home, and hardly consistent. But we do it.

I've had many different experiences teaching my children to read, and I'm not so sure there is "the way" that works for every child. One child picked it up on her own, quite early. Another worked through a workbook with me.[1] Another didn't get it until he began writing (first) through *Spell to Write and Read*.

SLOW SCHOOLING

Still another wasn't even motivated until she discovered Calvin and Hobbes. One of my daughters with Down syndrome is learning reading by sight. Patience, persistence, and perseverance. And modeling. My children see their mother and father read real books, too.

There are valid concerns with the content of books, and many times I have heard people insist that I must pre-read everything my children read. I find this amazing, as I have nine children, most of whom have ravenous reading habits like crows plowing through open corn fields. Furthermore, I simply do not have the funds (nor the desire) to create a bunker style home library. The best I have been able to do with this regard is to share lists of quality titles that I ask my children to read on a regular basis. Yes, they still may pick up a series of "candy" reading, but it works to set specific

TEACHING READING

books, authors, or genres as assigned reading as well. Also, when the Word is shared on a daily basis, children quickly see quite clearly reading material that would be shameful to set ones mind and eyes upon. Unfortunately, due to misguided "open access" to children, even pornographic novels are within reach in our community library. This is simply yet one more land mine with which to warn and teach our children about. Creating the illusion that (a) nothing is good "out there" or that (b) our home is "sinless" is not only untrue, but ripe for the call of hypocrisy. The Bible—and common sense—is clear here: there is no end to the making of books and there is no way we can absorb them all or preview everything our child comes across. Better to teach them how to discern good reading material, and then they will know.

SLOW SCHOOLING

Naturally, reading happens across the subjects taught in homeschooling. There is ample, good quality literature that very clever people have threaded through lessons in science and history, and I have found those sorts of curriculum to be very valuable in our home.[2]

What about real concerns regarding physical limitations with reading? Of course, some of these are real and should be checked out by the proper offices. Sometimes a child may need glasses, other times a dietary change is needed. Other times, a child may have a real visual discrimination problem. These are challenges, but not impossible ones. With real determination (and the right help as needed), your child can learn to read.

TEACHING READING

BLOG

"Dogs, Books, and Herbs"

Wednesday, August 1, 2007, 11:21pm

Let's talk about the avalanches of books we have everywhere. My hubby and I love books, and thus our children are already doomed. I decided to just go around to their bedsides and take a count. That was the least frustrating action I could take at the moment. The 3-year-old had eleven books in her bed, as did her 5-year-old sister. Already that's 22 books in one room. Add the 4 their big 9-year-old sister had, and voila, 26 books. Into the boys room, I counted one in the baby's bed, and...ready for this?...22 books for my 7-year-old son. TWENTY-TWO...5 on his bed, 6 underneath,

SLOW SCHOOLING

4 on the floor, and 7 piled on his bedside table.

So they like to read! But come now, how many books can you read at one time?

Ummm...let's see...I count 7 books and 2 magazines on my hubby's side table, and 12 near mine. Hmm....

16

Teaching History, Science, and Math

BLOG

"65 Sheets of Cardstock..."

Thursday, August 09, 2007, 02:54pm

And 158 staples (minus a few dozen mishaps) later, we finally have our timeline on the wall. I've been wanting to do this for years, and I took the opportunity today to just do it while a video babysat my 3-year-old and dreams played upon my wee one's naptime.

SLOW SCHOOLING

History, science, and math are blatant proclaimers of worldview. Depending on the foundation an instructor may attempt to construct, a child might learn that world history is millions of years old. Or that his ancestor was an ape. Or that history is measured in political and geographical upheavals, and that science is supposedly at odds with religion and mathematics is a tool of oppression.[1] Truth is presented in many history books in the measure and flavors of whomever the publishing house wishes to market to, and science books speak of evolution as fact, even though the very essence of science is based on the repeatable and observable. Science has become the god of our day, even though it is never going to be able to give a once and final answer to anything at all.

Thankfully, homeschooling allows our students to be honest about their starting points,

TEACHING HISTORY, SCIENCE, MATH

their presuppositions. If a child knows the Bible as the infallible Word of God, then of course history, archeology, and science will confirm that belief. If a child is in rebellion to the obvious and clear proofs all around him that God exists, then he will seek out every theory and premise that attacks what the Bible says, no matter how outlandish. Space aliens birthing the human race? Of course! Dinosaurs dying out millions of years ago? Naturally! And as promised in the Bible, this sort of dishonesty is rooted well in the sinful man who will not repent, and he will move yet further and further from the light of truth and come up with even more fantastic ideas.

Both subjects are steeped (or ought to be) in the pursuit of truth and in an honest assessment of what has transpired before, and what we can observe in the here and now. Understanding

SLOW SCHOOLING

at least a smidge of history and science (these are truly lifelong pursuits) helps a person to understand the world a little better, and to understand his or her place in it. And, obviously, God wants us to know history because the Bible is so full of historical references, places and people, and because He shows Himself in relation to those events and people in many ways. God also wants us to know science because we can see clearly so many evidences of His design. When we study history or science or even mathematics, we are studying His hand in all of everything and everyone for all time.

Clearly, the best history book is the Bible. The Bible is full of historical, geographical, and economical accounts and lessons. It teaches what is wise, and what is foolish, government and it lays out the foundation for social justice and

TEACHING HISTORY, SCIENCE, MATH

human prospering. It not only also teaches about social institutions such as church and family, it addresses social problems and how to show compassion and provide solutions. It is not surprising to see such pain in the world with such a low view of scripture alongside it.

Certainly, there are many books both for children and adults that add value to history studies, but none will surpass the study and understanding of the Bible. Biographies, textbooks, and even historical fiction may bring many interesting and relevant insights, but understanding the timeline of history as brought forth by the Bible will give every student a permanent footing in the subject. We have appreciated *Beautiful Feet Books* for matching literature with history studies.

SLOW SCHOOLING

Likewise, there is no shortage of science in the Bible! The Bible touches on many topics: astronomy, earth science, physics, chemistry, zoology, botany, human biology and life sciences.[2] Many of these subjects can be pursued as interested throughout the homeschooling years, with various textbooks, lab work and field trips. As students gain in maturity and study skills, they can study these topics more in depth with a trusted resource that not only does not deny the obvious truth of God and His creation, but honors the academic pursuits of excellence. Our family has used and appreciated *Apologia Science* and *Answers in Genesis* for their outstanding curriculums, but we have also used books such as *Botany in a Day* (giving room to discuss the evolutionary bias in it) and Comstock's *Nature Study* as textbooks. In addition, we are thankful for the teachers we have paid to teach advanced

TEACHING HISTORY, SCIENCE, MATH

courses with lab work. Homeschooling does not mean a parent needs to know everything or teach everything!

Mathematics is important as it also shows, for example, the handiwork of God, how orderly and dependable He is, and how concerned He is with right measurements. How interesting it is to see college students today on campus seeking engineering degrees arguing how two plus two could possibly equal seven, should you think that is right (and who are we to say anything is wrong?).[3] Our family has used many mathematic curriculums and helps: general workbooks for our youngers, *Teaching Textbooks* for our middles, and *Life of Fred* for our olders. We have also used *Math U See* for other students in our household.

SLOW SCHOOLING

Every child learns differently; part of the beauty of homeschooling is having the freedom to discover what works best.

These subjects are clearly important, but not because of how they might further a career or the pursuit of collegiate degrees. They are important because of what they teach about the world and about God. And once a child gets a good taste of how good the Lord is, even through these subjects, blessed will that child be!

17

Teaching the Fine Arts

"Thank Goodness I was never sent to school; it would have rubbed off some of the originality."

— Beatrix Potter

BLOG
"Drawing...or...How to Torture Your Kids"
Tuesday, April 8, 2008, 02:27pm

There was much weeping and gnashing of teeth this morning. We started our drawing lessons and you'd think I was asking my children to walk over hot coals in their bare tootsies.

I was quite nonchalant about the whole deal, and told them we were going to do some drawing lessons, which got the eager response I was hoping for. That response lasted until I gave them their initial assignments, which was to be baseline products to compare with later. OH, the gut-wretching cries! I can't draw! It looks horrible! I want a bigger eraser! And, did I mention, I CAN'T DRAW!!

"The process of learning to draw creates quite a lot of mental conflict."
   - Betty Edwards, *Drawing on the Right Side of the Brain*

TEACHING the FINE ARTS

Well, yep. Sure does! And after going through the process, the thought that stuck in my own mind was, "Wow...we are SO going to do this." I am looking forward to watching my children (and hopefully myself) grow and learn and awaken new levels of creativity. If my children at the ages of 6, 8, and 10 already think they "can't" draw, then something's amiss and it needs to be addressed!

I recently visited a beautiful university campus, and throughout the tour all of the amenities were highlighted: small classroom sizes, beautiful research facilities, and even organic offerings at the student cafe. The campus boasted not one, but two, large gymnasiums and plenty of outdoor fields and trails for athletic and physical education and enjoyment. While walking through another beige hallway (screaming for a mural, in my mind), I asked our tour guide, "What about the arts? Do you have a music program?" The answer was no. Should I send my son there, he'd have to put away his cello, but he could play rugby instead.

Physical education is not unimportant, and athletic competition offers many life lessons such as self-discipline, setting goals, and working with others to achieve goals. However, it does not equate that the arts ought to be first on the peg of cuts whenever funds dry up or unaddressed when yet another potential sport is brought to the table of ideas. Nor should it be last on the list of homeschooling goals, an add-on "if" the other subjects are all accounted for.

TEACHING the FINE ARTS

We are inherently creative because our Maker is creative. He created the entire world and all that is in it, and His creation offers us beauty, enjoyment, and instruction.[1] We, too, as part of His handiwork, reflect creativity when we express ourselves in whatever manner to bring out our own inner emotions, whether it be by dancing, gardening, painting, speaking, decorating (cakes or houses), tailoring, writing, or playing a musical instrument. We are creative when we organize our households or our work spaces, when we put together a lovely meal, or smooth out the bedsheets to make it an invitation come evening. We show that we are creative when we appreciate the colors of a sunset, keep beat to a piece of music, or doodle on our grocery lists.

So why do we keep these creative endeavors as "extras?" As we know from other areas of our lives, promising to get to them "tomorrow" or even "next year" does not always mean that we will. Instead, I would encourage a parent to make the creative arts something that is part of a regular routine.

The easiest place to begin is with a child's innate interest or curiosity with a particular creative art form. Does your child like to sing in a play microphone? Or play puppet theater? Or paint, sew, or hammer? Most children, if given the opportunity to play with a variety of possibilities, will naturally veer towards something they enjoy more than the others. Then, it is simply a matter of ensuring that the child has the time and space to play with those materials. You could take those interests even further with finding a particular book, course, class, or private tutor to either develop them

TEACHING the FINE ARTS

into something richer or reveal that it was simply a passing curiosity.

But what if a child's only interest is in which screen show to watch next, or to make the high score on a popular video game? I would strongly caution against feeding this appetite, for it is never appeased. Furthermore, although the child's brain and spirit may feel the high effect of doing a job well done for achieving a high score, the truth is that nothing of value or permanence was accomplished, and nothing was developed that would be a blessing to his or her family or community at large. Participating in such activities for a little down time is certainly not a sin, but it can be detrimental to a child's character and skill development over time.

SLOW SCHOOLING

What if a child simply shrugs about what he or she might enjoy doing? This is a problem easily remedied! Peruse the nonfiction shelves at the library: how to build airplanes, how to weave baskets, what native plants can be foraged and eaten, how to draw birds or do geometrical math puzzles. What makes the child say, "Ooh! THAT seems cool!" and simply pile up half a dozen books on the subject.

Another possibility is to participate with groups such as Trail Life for boys[2] or American Heritage Girls for (you guessed it) girls.[3] When our older children were younger, our family ran Keepers of the Faith club (now closed), in which children were able to choose from a variety of activities to try and earn badges on. All of these are helpful for trying out different activities and seeing what is interesting and possible.

TEACHING the FINE ARTS

One of the great benefits of homeschooling is that field trips can happen often! These can be trips to museums, art galleries, botanical lectures, music events, theater events, aquariums, farms, and even behind the scenes to in-town places such as the post office and grocery store. I fondly remember in childhood watching my Greek grandmother feeding the chickens, my mother doing needlework, and being fascinated by women at the county fair spinning wool with their wheels: these are activities I have enjoyed as an adult. Give your child many different experiences. You never know what will "stick" in adulthood, and to be sure it may not be the carefully curated curriculum that you personally chose!

In thinking about what is necessary for life and godliness, I would urge you not to forsake the arts. Make art class a requirement, for example.[4] I would also urge you to provide your students with real tools, not toys. Just like the art of creating a meal is far more pleasurable and easier with good knives, painting is more pleasurable with rich pigmented paints and easier with good quality brushes. It's dishonest to say you "tried" sewing and hated it if the only equipment you attempted to use were dull needles and faded or fraying threads. Buy the best quality tools you can afford.

Lastly, at risk of sounding repetitive, you cannot give what you do not have. Consider how YOU are expressing your own creative bents. Do you knit? Cook? Do any woodworking? Garden, play music, or even make rope? Do your children know and see that you are interested in the world, God's creative handiwork, is fascinating? Do you buy or check

TEACHING the FINE ARTS

out books from the library on a variety of subjects? Some children will naturally be drawn to the creative arts, others may need more of an invitation. We as adults might do well to consider where we might be on that continuum, too, so that we can reflect our Father's creative side as well.

18

Real Life Helps Along the Way

Because homeschooling, and especially slow schooling, is not simply (simply!) about trying to cram as much knowledge into a child as possible in the shortest time given, it might be prudent to consider other aspects of home life that weave throughout the day and add to a child's instruction and character building. If a child grows up to speak eloquently and perform beautifully, but never prays to God or spends a moment of time with his grandmother, of what use was his training? Education is not at the top an academic affair; it is an affirmation of the child as a whole and dignified human being with much to offer in every area of life, at all ages of life.

Scheduling

I am very grateful for the work of Teri Maxwell and her *Managers of the Home* workbook. Every few months I reassess how our routines are working, and we try again with a new schedule or simply tweak areas that are not working. Going through the process is always a blessing, and the reason I am able to blog, quilt, study, or even take a nap, is because we do the best we can to keep on a schedule. That being said, we never (no, not once) are able to keep to it 100%. I am never good at making hard stops, and my transition times are

REAL LIFE HELPS ALONG the WAY

always fluid. I truly use this scheduling process as a foundation, and then let our routines settle in the most comfortable ways for us. Every family (and their specific challenges) are different. I would encourage you, especially if you feel overwhelmed or have too many discipline issues, to try this system out, but remember that a schedule is not your master, it is simply a tool.

Toddlers

Toddlers love to "do school" along with their older siblings, but it is true that after about 15 minutes at the table, they are ready to run off! Having a schedule (as above) helps tremendously in keeping them safe, happy, and busy. It is helpful to rotate activities, books, and toys, as well as having outdoor play and a nap or rest time every day. It is simply not true that they need many of their own age-mates to play with on a regular basis; what they need is a predictable environment with the family they love and plenty of opportunities to explore, create, and grow.

Finances

The most difficult part of financing homeschooling books and supplies is seeing thousands of dollars in tax money leave our family's pockets to fund the school down the street, while I try to scrape together a few hundred dollars for curriculum. Having had experience in the public school systems and observing how money was spent there make it an especially bitter pill, but we honestly never are without learning opportunities and a

REAL LIFE HELPS ALONG the WAY

library. Furthermore, the younger children were able to use books the older children are finished with, so the cost of materials simply gets less as time goes on.

Sometimes families feel compelled to join up with the public school system in a "partnership" to get extra funds for computers, music lessons, and the like. I would strongly discourage this. Not only do you lose your status as an independent homeschooler (your child becomes, basically, a public school student, working from home), but it puts at risk the opportunity for others in the future to homeschool. Should the Lord agree that music lessons are what your child needs, I have full faith that He would provide the means for you to procure them. Be well advised that public schools embark in this sort of partnership not for the good of your child, but for the federal money in their

SLOW SCHOOLING

accounts and the educational control you would begin to relinquish.[1]

Also, it is often tempting, if not necessary, to consider that a second parent bring an income to support the family economy. I would urge you to be honest about what your real needs are; having a roof of simple shingle over your head isn't necessarily the same as having a roof of gold over your head. Do you need cable TV? A second car? The right brand of clothing? If after humble contemplation the need for further funds is an absolute necessity, I would encourage a family to consider what they might do as a family business from the home. The opportunities to make money through selling to a now global audience through the internet is vast and promising to anyone willing to put in the hard work of learning the ropes.

REAL LIFE HELPS ALONG the WAY

Many parents are worried that they will not be able to afford college tuition. Again, I would encourage you to consider what your goals and efforts toward education are. If those goals make it absolutely necessary for your child to gain the colored rope, there are many opportunities to do so outside of a brick and mortar building, such as online distance learning. Many high schoolers participate in dual enrollment, completing their diploma along with a couple of years of college work at a tremendously discounted rate. I would, however, exercise caution if dual enrollment involves becoming a public school student for the reasons already brought forth.

HOMEMAKING

Homemaking is an inevitable part of homeschooling, for better or for worse. For better, in that children have more time and opportunity to take on the responsibilities of caring for the home through chores. And for worse, because the house never gets a break from all of the people in it, so keeping it tidy is akin to shoveling sidewalks while snow is still falling. Scheduling chores and even meal plans has helped me tremendously, and I am grateful to Fly Lady for the push and homework I needed to get me going.[2] When the children were younger, we made games of cleaning up, such as "horse race clean up" where Daddy would play announcer and the "horses" would explode from the gates to pick up all of the toys they could. The "races" became a famous, and favorite, activity.

REAL LIFE HELPS ALONG the WAY

Drug-Free Health

With so much media and societal pressure to push drugs, it's no wonder a parent is rowing upstream to raise a drug-free family. However, given that properly prescribed prescription drugs are the fourth leading cause of death (more than 290 people every day)[3] and that 1 in 4 children suffer from allergies, 1 in 12 have asthma, and 1 in 36 have autism,[4] it is simply a matter of life and death to make wise decisions in how we treat the various symptoms we have or to prevent them from occurring. I define "drug-free" as eating foods grown without pesticides and living a lifestyle that includes chiropractic adjustments, good sleep hygiene and regular times of outdoor play, even barefoot. When symptoms do arise, we make use of homeopathic remedies and herbs. I encourage you to make use of the many classes in first aid (CPR, etc) and alternative methods of gently healing, including use of people, physicians, and dentists who are integrative and holistic.

Media

It's no secret anymore that media is a powerful venue for the formation of minds and culture. It's also very evident that few people are able to resist the siren call of amusing themselves to death[5] as seen in the gross number of hours spent on social media and other entertainments. It's not a shock anymore to see blasphemy, violence, sultry images, or to read stunning and vicious comments by people who may, in real life, be polite in the grocery store. Pornography robs and enslaves millions of people every year, both by permission and by force. With smart

REAL LIFE HELPS ALONG the WAY

phones ubiquitous and iPads in the hands of toddlers, it does seem like a tsunami of sin and sadness, destroying dreams, goals, innocence, and even the humanity of individual people. Fifteen years of life sunk away into the TV alone.[6] What are we missing?

Of course, these tools can be helpful and a blessing, but therein lies the caution: they CAN be. Much like an electric fence, the purpose may be proper, but a careless application can be deadly. It's completely unrealistic to shield our children completely from the internet (or public libraries, for that matter), but we must thoughtfully protect them and prepare them.

We got rid of our TV in 2009, and have rarely thought twice about it. What I miss about it is the excitement of waiting all year to watch "Frosty the Snowman" and my brother and I skidding to land on our bottoms ready for the show when CBS trumpeted its announcement. Sunday evenings were similar, with Tinker Bell flying about the castle heralding the family-friendly movie of the week. In the background, my dad had the paper nearby, and my mom worked on needlepoint.

Because of this technology propelling a proud individualism, it is unnecessary now to spend any time together for a shared experience. In fact, it's unnecessary to spend any time alone either, in boredom. Boredom used to be where imagination and rest did their best work. Instead, we practice escapism, neglect honing our crafts, and forgo real face-to-face hospitality. Parents are altogether too eager to use the "plug-in drug" because it is easier to administer than creative play, diligent work, or

REAL LIFE HELPS ALONG the WAY

character-building discipline. We all know this is harmful, intuitively.

Furthermore, screen time has real health concerns: loss of short-term memory, distracted driving, radiation.[7] No one is, in fact, heralding these tools as beneficial for the body, soul, and mind, but plenty will fight to the death to avoid going without one. Try even one day without your smart phone and see for yourself if you hunger for a screen swipe, a check in to Twitter, or agonize over unseen email. This is the world our children are growing up in and will more than likely end up with if we do nothing: addicted and narcissistic, where their sense of accomplishment is measured by the high score or the number of followers.

SLOW SCHOOLING

I encourage you and your family to be mindful of media choices. Decide what tools you will use, make sure your children know how and when to use them, and also to know WHY your particular rules are there. It is not negligent nor unkind to withhold cell phones or the nightly newscast, or to stall opening their email or social media accounts. Plan, and take, regular media fasts. Set individual and family goals for the next year, and beyond.[8] Teach them to recognize predators, spam, and questionable websites or communications. One thing is for certain: if you desire your children to know the screen as a tool and not as a master, you must lead by example in this area. Otherwise you are greatly deceived by its power and your own enslavement to it.[9]

REAL LIFE HELPS ALONG the WAY

Toys and Play

Toys don't have to be a hinderance to curiosity or an irritation to the household: a hinderance, by means of battery-powered (versus brain-powered) construction, and/or an irritation, by means of, well, battery-powered (versus gross or fine motor-powered), play. It's no secret in my home that as far as toys go, I plainly prefer simple over complex, wooden over plastic, and quality over quantity. I also find the idea that a noisy mechanized voice wobbling out what are supposed to be phonograms so that children can learn to more readily read is foolishness. What they need is a good book on a loving lap.

Because toys are one means of creative play and learning, they are important in the home. However, many toys on the market today, especially geared to babies, are actually burdensome or even harmful to a small child's immune system. How so? BPA is a chemical compound found in many plastic products, and it's recognized to have estrogenic activity, disrupting normal endocrine and reproductive function...and it's allowed in pacifiers, teethers, and toys. It leaches out of the plastic (and into your children) through everyday use.[10] It is not "over the top" to request wooden trains instead of plastic ones; it is simply attempting to raise a healthy child. There are many other chemical concoctions that can also be avoided by using more natural products for play things, such as rubber, wood, or wool. The bacteria on wooden surfaces don't multiply; they simply die. [11] Consider that when high chair shopping, too.

Thanks to the internet, providing these toys are not that difficult to find. However, they come at a cost. A plastic, $3 rattle is more

REAL LIFE HELPS ALONG the WAY

appealing to the pocketbook than a wooden, $17 one. If you look beyond the cost, however, what you will also see is that the wooden rattle will last, well, forever. Furthermore, anyone concerned with consumerism and materialism will agree that cheaper toys won't become valuable just because you buy MORE of them. Better quality and fewer toys is one aspect that makes for a home that everyone can enjoy and live in.

Exceptions to the "rule" in our home? Lego bricks are the most obvious, being plastic AND excessive. Lego definitely has made the "lasts forever" check! Also, gifts are generally accepted, but are the first to get weeded out if inappropriate or unplayed with. Other toys that have real staying power throughout the years include bicycles and wagons, art supplies, dolls,

SLOW SCHOOLING

balls, tools (yes, REAL tools, not "play" tools), little cars and a (wood) play kitchen.

Let's not, however, come up with a "must have" list. Our children have owned a McMansion-sized playset, but were just as enthusiastic with the milk crate and rope swing they made for themselves later. Giving a child training in the use of tools, access to the outdoors, and plenty of wood and other scraps is a recipe for the cultivation of a great, imaginary mind. No batteries or WiFi needed!

Actually, many useful "toys" are missing in this generation, such as rocks and sticks. Rocks—that children are no longer allowed to throw. Sticks—that children are no longer allowed to use as guns. Instead, we put an electronic device in their hands for "hand and eye coordination" and shrug when they lose their observational

REAL LIFE HELPS ALONG the WAY

and social skills. Other MIA toys include: small lenses and magnifying glasses to explore the undersides of plants and bugs, binoculars, pocket knives, spindles, shovels and mud. And proper training in using these things can only occur if a parent is willing to put down THEIR electronic device.

Which brings us to the most important "toy" of all: YOU. No matter what is going on in a child's day, no matter if he is drawing a comic strip or she is serving her dolly tea, there is no greater joy than having Daddy or Mommy join them in their play. Joining them does not necessarily mean directing them; it means allowing time to do creative play together. When you come home for the day, or even for a quick lunch, yes your children will be thrilled beyond measure if you jump into their inflatable pool with them fully dressed. Ask me how I know.

Do you want your children to play? Then you must play, too. Sometimes in order to rescue childhood you must be willing to rediscover a bit of yours. For how will your child readily believe their imagination is important if they never see you using yours? If going outside for fresh air and sunshine is so great, are you doing the same? Play has purpose beyond productivity.

Could you take an art class, just because? Show up for a Saturday night volleyball game? I'd encourage you to pick your own toys and hobbies wisely, as well as your child's, because they will enhance your own health and well being, too.

REAL LIFE HELPS ALONG the WAY

The Local Church

Attending a local church is a necessity for the Christian. Not only is it a place to meet, thereby not forsaking the assembling of others (Hebrews 10:25), it is also a place in which to partake of the sacraments of the Lord's Supper and baptism. With clear instructions on the qualifications of pastors, elders, and deacons, it is fairly obvious that God intended a structured gathering. Many people believe that they can simply listen to a sermon from a podcast and get good Bible teaching. Although this can be true, depending on who you are listening to, it is also true that that particular pastor in all of the study time he has put in to bring the message to his flock never once considered you specifically or your family. He doesn't know your life, your troubles, or how your walk with the Lord is going. This is actually part of the reason why people stay home; they want the invisibility. Belonging to a local church also means submitting yourself to church discipline, which is another reason people may shy from attending. Although it may be difficult to find a church that faithfully preaches the Word of God, it is worth the effort (perhaps even the move!), to belong to a larger family within the community, and this is of great benefit to our children as well.

Special Needs and Adoption

Children with special needs and children who have been adopted, at times, bring their own unique and difficult challenges. Regardless of how they are schooled, their family needs the love and active support of their church. I say "active" because many families dealing with

REAL LIFE HELPS ALONG the WAY

these challenges need more than advice—they need physical, mental, and emotional support. Not every adoptive or special needs parent struggles, but many parents sincerely—and quietly—do. They may hesitate to relay needs because (a) they may be judged as lacking in parenting skills (even if they're not) and/or (b) they do not want to discount the very real ways that God's grace has been shown through this time. However, with encouragement and tangible help, even these children can and do thrive with a home-based instruction and attention.

As a parent with two daughters with Down syndrome, I understand the reality of how difficult it is to ask for help, and the disappointment when it does not, or cannot, come. God's grace is truly sufficient during those times! If you are a parent without these challenges, and you know someone in your congregation with them, let me implore you: Ask how things are honestly going, listen, and believe whatever that parent tells you because some of the issues that may arise are truly horrific (especially in cases such as Reactive Attachment Disorder). Offer help in whatever way your family can manage. Could you relieve the family for a few hours for a break? Could you bless them out of the blue with a supper provided, or help clean their home, or help with a maintenance project that is weighing on them? Or perhaps you could gift money so that equipment and other ongoing extra costs might be less worrisome? Could you send them a card with scripture to brighten their day or to give them strength? Or offer to pray (and then do it!) for whatever that child's needs are? We all need to remember that they are a part of the church community and to do

REAL LIFE HELPS ALONG the WAY

what we can to lift what can sometimes be a tremendous burden—even a wee bit—so these children can benefit from slow schooling also.

On Finding a Mentor

As a younger mother, I prayed and pined for a godly mentor. I was hungry for that older woman of the Word who would come alongside and encourage me with the scriptures and with advice, who would rejoice in my growing family and help me with practicalities such as scheduling and homeschooling and homemaking. Unfortunately, none of the women I sought seemed to be available, and I shamefully went through a season of bitterness about it. Let me exhort you not to follow that same path!

SLOW SCHOOLING

There is nothing inherently wrong with desiring a mentor, and scripture actually commands the elder to teach the younger. Unfortunately, many of the older women in the church are of a generation that probably did not get that for themselves, so they feel ill equipped to offer any kind of leadership. They may have real regrets in their own mothering and cannot imagine why anyone would seek their counsel. Lastly, even if these women wholeheartedly love and support what you are doing in theory, practically speaking they may have become too busy in their own schedules to fit into yours.

On the other side, older women who desire to mentor the younger generation are sometimes hindered by a lack of real attentiveness or desire from that younger mother to learn. It is also true that many young women who say

REAL LIFE HELPS ALONG the WAY

they want mentoring do not want mentoring at all; they only want a coffee date in which they can vent all of their frustrations. This is a problem when a true mentor longs to guide a younger women through the Word, through prayer, Biblical counseling, and through lessons learned by experience, but the younger woman is too enamored by Pinterest-homemaking, current day child-raising practices, or by worldly notions of what marriage ought to look like.

Either woman in earnest ought to seek a fruitful match by prayer. In the meantime, if no mentor match is forthcoming, know that God's grace is sufficient! Many godly, older women have written books that are extremely valuable for the seeking younger mother, and if such a mother will slowly consider what it written (testing it by the Word of course), and will in earnestness apply what is there, there is no reason that woman can't grow in whatsoever she is currently struggling in and come to peace with her progress.

If you're longing for a mentor and cannot find one, endeavor to become the mentor you wish you had. Because it is true that the years fly by and one day you will look around and see younger mothers, with younger children...and they will be thirsty for a good word, even from you. Share it.

Keeping It in Perspective

Spring softly swept in, with patches of sun flashing through the windows between diagonal downpours. I sat with my ten and twelve-year-olds at the table, and in that 45 minutes or so, I oversaw their note taking, taught about exchanging Y for I in spelling words, and quizzed them on William Bradford and the multiplication tables. As they gathered up their daily planner and books, I swirled what was left of my latte. Was this enough? Am I doing enough? Are they getting enough?

SLOW SCHOOLING

It is the question that looms large at many homeschooling tables, and one that the secular world is quick to answer with a violent, "NO!" But it is the wrong question. It assumes that no educational institution (or parent, for that matter) will ever be enough, do enough. And it assumes that the child is a blank slate, without personality, interests, or needs that make him not only a unique individual, but...human.

Homeschooling, and specifically slow schooling, allows for children to blossom under the love and care of their family. It even allows the parent to blossom, allowing for their own pursuits in adding value to the family economy. There is a good balance of teaching and training in the areas of great importance to the family, and a freedom to explore and investigate areas of personal interest. The foundation to the slow school is the truth of

KEEPING IT in PERSPECTIVE

every individual being valuable as an image bearer of God. This brings about in society a real diversity, a real tolerance for difference, and a real love and respect for the honor and dignity every single person carries from the womb to the tomb.

Education is not something that takes place only during certain hours in certain places around certain age groups. Schooling as we currently know it attempts to funnel this bright range of humanity onto one track for one purpose: to forward the agenda of a cultural elite through the strength of propaganda and oppression of law. Allowing families the responsibility and joy of raising and educating their own children is an exercise in faith.

Slow schooling is not separate from life living. I'd like to encourage you to relax a little

SLOW SCHOOLING

if you are too high-strung about getting textbooks completed, especially in the younger (pre-high school-ish) years. And I'd like to also prod you to introduce curriculum that your children might never stumble upon on their own. Find a balance that is engaging, challenging, interesting, and fun. Concentrate more on cultivating an inquiring, intelligent mind than preparing for a career that may or may not even exist by the time your child reaches adulthood. Consider who you are hoping will benefit from that education, and how you might take joy in whatever vocation God seems to be setting before your child.

Lastly, it's crucial to maintain an eternal perspective on educating (and thereby discipling) your children. A hundred years from now, it will not matter how many good grades were recorded or even what kind of income

KEEPING IT in PERSPECTIVE

they grew up into earning for themselves. What ultimately matters is not only your faithfulness in teaching your children about God, but their faithfulness in responding to the gospel.

When you teach your children, you're essentially teaching your grandchildren. Do it wisely. May we all reach for that glorious endeavor to teach our children of the Lord, and may their peace (and yours) be great because of it.

"Slow School"
(The Original Blog Post)

BLOG

"Slow School"

Wednesday, June 10, 2015, 09:38am

While I was pregnant last fall, I had a woman ask about the number of children I had, and my age. I told her (smile). She shook her head when she inquired about homeschooling, proceeded to lament her teen son's apparent lack of educational ambitions, and then said, and I quote, "If I were

SLOW SCHOOLING

pregnant again you'd have to take me out to the woods and shoot me!"

Well. That's sad, on a whole lot of levels.

I wonder if sometimes having any children at all is just a matter of having something to check off on the list of life. Then we push them to grow up as fast as possible so that we can get to doing whatever it is we want to be doing instead of being with our babies. Or maybe we keep them home and homeschool but then we still push them to finish the textbook within an allotted time-frame so that we can get them to the next one this September so that they could hurry up and graduate and go to the proper college to get the

"SLOW SCHOOL" (The Original Blog Post)

job that will, again, allow us to get to doing whatever it is we want to be doing instead. (You can ask your kid to diagram that last sentence. You're welcome).

How come just being with these little people isn't enough?

I guess I'm wondering what the point is. Is the point just to have children, get them educated, and then…whatever…? What's the rush? And what's wrong with a 40-something-year-old woman having (a)nother baby? (Or does that only work if I put in 20 years into another career first)?

I'm wondering why learning can't just be another aspect of living. Like eating. Can you imagine

SLOW SCHOOLING

finishing up a good lunch, and before your lips swipe the napkin already fretting about the next meal, when it will be, how much time it might take, if the ingredients are all there, and *what if* it doesn't assuage your hunger? But there we are as homeschoolers, already plotting and planning the curriculum for the next umpteen years even as our babies are just learning to read, fretting about *what if* we mess up their lives by choosing the wrong math book.

Are you struggling with this? I don't have a website or book or method to recommend. You might laugh at what I recommend, and it is this: relax, already. As in, just park for a few minutes a day

"SLOW SCHOOL" (The Original Blog Post)

and read a book to your child without wondering if it's on the list of must-reads in order for your 8-year-old to set sail for AP English later on. Because, frankly, your child might not want to go to college. Your child might want to run a landscaping business because he likes the outdoors. Or maybe swing a hammer. Or be a farmer. You do like pretty parks, right? You like living in a house? You like eating? Someone had to plant the plants, build the house, grow the food. Why not let your child bloom into his or her own interests?

Too many times, too many years, we press them into our own educational biases before we give them a chance to learn about

SLOW SCHOOLING

what they're interested in. Or we drag them to this and that when they just want to stay home or go fishing.

Many people ask about our homeschool, and I guess I've hesitated in sharing because it can be a contentious subject. But I think I've outgrown the comparison dance and my skin's grown thick enough to withstand the withering opinions of others. We do other things than just "schoolwork". We play. We play music. We do chores, bake, and take care of chickens. We ride bikes, play with Lego (a lot), and keep the sewing machines humming. Sometimes we act in theater productions, sometimes we dissect frogs with friends, and we are

"SLOW SCHOOL" (The Original Blog Post)

constantly putting books on hold from the library. And reading them. In other words, we just live life. And, somehow, perhaps miraculously, they learn stuff. And I have the test results to prove it

I've dabbled in many different schooling methods over the years (my eldest is now 17 1/2). First of course was the school-at-home method, because that is what I knew both from being a graduate of AND an educator in the public school system. That was insanely stressful, because everything else in our lives rotated around the schoolwork. I wanted learning to be in every part of our lives, not just from this hour to that one. Recently, maybe it was the

SLOW SCHOOLING

downsize, maybe it was the massive decluttering of not just stuff but of our lives, but I like where our homeschool is nowadays. It is, for lack of a better word, relaxed. Comfortable. Easy-going, and yet very productive and fun. It feels right. It is furthering one of my Big Goals: raising kids who not only know *how* to learn but *want* to learn. That will fit them for life rather well, I think.

Each of my kids has a planner. I ask them at the beginning of the day what they are *planning* to do that day. It's a good way to check on chores (laundry day, for example), and I can also keep them moving along with whatever subject ("let's see a couple of math pages

"SLOW SCHOOL" (The Original Blog Post)

done today"). Just the act of writing down their *plans* means that it is all more likely to get done. They're aware of the day and their goals, and it keeps them on track. I also like that it puts the onus of learning on THEM. What I say around here is that it is MY responsibility to provide materials and to teach, but it is THEIR responsibility to learn. Furthermore, once a kid gets an idea they're excited about ("I want to work for NASA!"), then the planner is a slam dunk: "Ok, then, let's look at what their requirements are…oh, you need a degree in something like mathematics…which means, you'll need to take these classes…." Then, when we're dealing with an unmotivated slug, I can shrug and

SLOW SCHOOLING

say, "That's ok…it just means it will take you longer to get to NASA…and do your math anyway…."

We try to get some homeschooling done every day, all year round. I could say, not including weekends, but that would be false, because my kids love to read and learn and I'm not about to ban them from books on certain days of the week. Like I said, it's just living. Like eating. We eat on weekends, too.

So I guess my method right now is "slow school." I dunno if that's trademarked yet, but you (maybe) heard it here first :). Here are some things we do in our homeschool, and some ideas for you to consider. Every day is

"SLOW SCHOOL" (The Original Blog Post)

blessedly different, and I don't fret if we do less on one day than another. It just sort of all works out and I'm not spending a bazillion hours anymore "planning".

Ideas for Daily and Weekly Slow School:

[refer to Endnotes, Links, & References]

You know, you only have today. Yesterday is gone and tomorrow is just a wish. And children are a blessing, and that means even while they are at our feet…or in the womb. Enjoy them! And no, I'm not *announcing* anything ;)

Happy (and relaxed) learning!

Extras

This book was inspired by the article I wrote in the previous chapter some time ago by the same name—primarily because it resonated with so many. As I began to think how I might expand the concept into a book, I realized as I poured over my blog archives that I *already* have. The idea of "Slow Schooling" is a recurring theme, interwoven in my writings of "A Happy Home." Below are some "extra" excerpts from my writings that didn't necessarily find themselves in the final draft of this book. Nonetheless, may you find encouragement and blessing from them.

– *KML*

SLOW SCHOOLING

BLOG

"Our Open House 2008: Part 1"
Saturday, August 20, 2008, 02:21pm

As I've gotten older and have some half dozen years of homeschooling now behind me, I have realized that schooling at home is not anything more spectacular than, say, feeding my family or keeping the house in order. Preparing breakfast is just something that needs to be done...so is reading to the children. Sanitizing the bathrooms is important...so is teaching my children to count change.

But occasionally ***homeschooling*** becomes this monstrous impossibility of trying to translate romantic notions of

EXTRAS

gently and purposefully feeding our children's minds with the very best of one or more philosophical bents, such as Charlotte Mason, Classical, or Traditional. Of course, there are "right" ways and "wrong" ways to approach each of these, with the "proper" books and curriculum, and if by chance we mess it up (which of course, no public or private school teacher would ever do, har har har), the year and age of opportunity are gone, gone, gone and we have no one to blame but ourselves.

Ack! Is it any wonder we moms can freak out come September?

If I could...I'd like to earnestly encourage homeschooling mothers to just RELAX, to enjoy life with

SLOW SCHOOLING

their children, to think of schooling as just another facet of homelife and not as an "extra" thing to do in addition to everything else. It isn't any more "extra" than doing laundry.

Unless of course you usually hire out a laundress to do your dirty work.

I'd encourage you to sell or put away the curriculum or textbooks that you now know were a mistake for your family, not to feel guilty and thus plow through it simply because you spent money on it. After all, if something spoils in the fridge, are you going to eat it anyway—only because you spent money on it? We need to give ourselves grace, to know that

EXTRAS

homeschooling (like everything else) will never be perfect and that errors will happen. You can start "fresh" at any time, whether it be September, Thursday or the middle of an afternoon. It's no big deal. Tie up the laces anew and get back to walking.

I'd also encourage you to foster a love of learning through example (do YOU read?), and to shorten those intense lesson times. Make playing outside a priority, and take care with food choices and times for rest. If you have a child who would rather climb the roof, make instructional table time short (like 15-20 minutes) at a time. You know what excites your children; use these things to your advantage to teach them. Four

SLOW SCHOOLING

hours of pencil and paper work is NOT more advantageous than four hours of imaginative play.

And yes, learning anything at all takes a bit of pain (try learning another hand skill or another language as an adult!) But, again, it is by our example that our children will learn the best lessons: perseverance, hard work, a good attitude. We can't expect them to rise above our own example.

EXTRAS

BLOG

"Learning Happens"

Wednesday, September 5, 2007, 08:17am

It's so great that I don't have to plan for my children's every learning experience. What I am finding more and more, is that I just have to get out of the way (ie. RELAX) and let them have at it. During recent lunchtime conversations alone, we've talked genetics, fractions and parts of speech, all brought up from stuff the kiddos have been reading about on their own. How cool is that?!

Here is my 5-year-old daughter's copywork, unassigned by me. Copywork is a very effective way to practice handwriting, learn grammar, and grow in vocabulary.

SLOW SCHOOLING

She is so excited to be reading and writing, that she just began to copy books on her own...Here are my daughters (3yo, 5yo, 9yo), busy washing and putting out to dry dolly clothes. I loved hearing them so involved with one another, and they were so proud of their work. I am still trying to convince my eldest that the laundry machine really is far better than hand-washing.

And here is my 7-year-old son, learning how to use power tools under the watchful eye of his dad...And here is the rabbit hutch they built, all from scrap material....

My children are all gaining confidence in their abilities,

EXTRAS

learning real life skills, and bonding with their family members. I wish I could take credit for all of that; truly, glory belongs to God. That, and thankfulness that I can have a front-row-seat to watch it all unfold.

BLOG

"A Peek Into Our Homeschool"

Monday, August 20, 2007, 08:14am

[From a another blogger's interview of my homeschool]

Q: Do you homeschool in a homeschool room, at the kitchen table, at a desk, in the park on the grass?

A: *Yes.*

SLOW SCHOOLING

Q: Do you have any "must share" tips?

A: *Yes! RELAX! Your children WILL learn, on their own timeframe. Read to them a lot, give them love and discipline, manage their chores, and let them be themselves. Play with them, and pray with them. And always, always, point them to God.*

Q: Do you have a question or concern? Throw that in there too!

A: *Am I doing a good job? Am I ruining my children? Why didn't I...? How come I can't...? Can we start over? What do I do about...? Can't someone come SHOW me how to...? And can I be reimbursed for all the stuff I bought that I-never-use-but-had-to-have-because-*

EXTRAS

everyone-else-loved-it??...Oh, the questions never end! Even though I *know* my children belong at home, I am forever hopeful that I won't screw them up. I am at peace, however, knowing that God will not only lead me in training them up, He will stand in the gaps (the enormous, gaping holes) to work out His plan in drawing them to Himself. And that, most of all, is the reward and pleasure of watching them grow and learn.

On Being "Called" to...(fill in the blank)

I humbly submit this blog post I wrote after the birth of our first (of two) daughters born with Down syndrome. If you'd like to hear the story

SLOW SCHOOLING

of either (or both) of their births and the effect on our family, I'd encourage you to check out the podcasts my husband and I did.[1] Homeschooling has continued through every trial our family has faced, because life is not all about academics, but about glorifying God in every way we are able, including academics. May we look to walk faithfully in ALL areas of our lives.

BLOG

"Chosen?"

Friday, June 27, 2008, 02:57pm

> "We will see more and more that we are chosen, not because of our ability, but because of His power that will be demonstrated in our not being able."
>
> — Corrie Ten Boom

EXTRAS

There runs a familiar story of somehow being specially chosen to raise a special child because somehow I (or whomever else gifted with such challenges) have more to offer than the ordinary Jane. It embraces the common notion that "the Lord does not give you anything more than you can handle," to which I cannot help but reply, "Wanna bet?"

The way I see it goes somewhat like this: if indeed the Lord does not ever give me more than I can handle, then truly I have no need of His direction, strength or loving exhortation. After all, if my own hands are fully equipped to the task I am facing, what need have I of His? Nay, friends, I humbly disagree. My Father in

SLOW SCHOOLING

heaven will ask me to do much beyond my abilities, my confidences, my understandings. For it is in through such overwhelming and ridiculous odds that I am certain to stumble at best and utterly fail at worst that God will Himself show up. I have to believe it is thus, for if I do not, then I am doomed to despair. I am doomed to bury myself in the multitudes of counselors. I am doomed to chase after every idea and help that my finite mind is invited to partake in, and that in turn will lead me helter-skelter spiritually, physically and emotionally as well.

I feel the pull already. The literature I read exhorts me to

EXTRAS

act now, to find immediate early intervention, to make decisions that even will affect my daughter's future as an adult. This is hard for me. I am more ponderous, more thoughtful, more careful. I feel more apt to simply stay put, to continue to teach her how to nurse without bruising her mama's tender parts, and to allow my own body to recover from surgery. Is it wrong to sit with her out in the garden for now, enjoying the sun and the wispy breeze, watching the dragonflies and swallows do acrobatics in the clear, blue sky?

I reject the notion that I have been "called" to be a mother, simply because I now have six children, or that I am "called" to

have this special child. What I
have been called to from the
beginning is only to faithfulness.
Faith grows from responding to and
trusting His heart, that even when
His ways and commands seem
nonsensical, we know them to be
not burdensome.

I know I have been given much to
carry. I know I am not equipped. I
do not share the delusion that
somehow I am more ready, eager, or
willing to take on the hard things
presented to me. All I have, all I
want to have, is trust that God is
indeed bigger, and to know He is
willing and able to lead me.

EXTRAS

Cause me to know the way wherein I should walk; for I lift up my soul unto Thee.

(Psalm 143:8)

I will guide thee with mine eye.

(Psalm 32:8)

Endnotes, Links, & References

Preface

1. https://www.thinkimpact.com/homeschooling-statistics/ —accessed October 17, 2021 (Definitely take the time to read these stats!)

Start Here

1. http://www.recognizetrauma.org/statistics.php — accessed August 22, 2016

2. http://news.sky.com/story/babies-born-hooked-on-heroin-special-report-10347175 —accessed August 22, 2016

3. http://www.nbcnews.com/business/business-news/things-are-looking-americas-porn-industry-n289431 —accessed August 22, 2016

4. http://www.dailymail.co.uk/news/article-2176281/Generation-refuse-grow-No-mortgage-No-marriage-No-children-No-career-plan-Like-30-somethings-Marianne-Power-admits-shes-.html – accessed August 22, 2016

5. http://www.bigfishgames.com/blog/2015-global-video-game-stats-whos-playing-what-and-why/ – accessed August 22, 2016

6. https://www.washingtonpost.com/business/economy/the-big-business-behind-the-adult-coloring-book-craze/2016/03/09/ccf241bc-da62-11e5-891a-4ed04f4213e8_story.html – accessed August 22, 2016

7. http://www.cnn.com/2016/08/21/asia/turkey-wedding-explosion/ – accessed August 22, 2016

8. Child suicide bomber kills 5 at Afghan wedding. July 12, 2019. https://apnews.com

Chapter 1: Schooling vs. Education

1. An example of the success of early homeschoolers: Rudner. The Scholastic

ENDNOTES, LINKS, & REFERENCES

Achievement and Demographic Characteristics of Home School Students. 1998.

Chapter 2: The Real World
1. https://www.amblesideonline.org/CMAttainments.shtml—accessed August 22, 2016
2. John Taylor Gatto, American author and school teacher: https://en.wikipedia.org/wiki/John_Taylor_Gatto
3. Suicide was the leading cause of death for those aged 10 to 19 in Japan in 2014. The intensity of the competitive school environment was listed as one trigger. (*Tackling the deadliest day for Japanese teenagers.* BBC News 08/31/2015. https://bbc.com/news/word-asia-34105044)

Chapter 3: What Slow School is NOT
1. http://www.holtgws.com/whatisunschoolin.html —accessed August 31, 2016

SLOW SCHOOLING

Chapter 4: What Slow School IS

1. http://www.albertmohler.com/2016/01/20/the-scandal-of-biblical-illiteracy-its-our-problem-4/ – accessed August 30, 2016

2. I am deeply indebted to Ruth C. Haycock and her series of books *Encyclopedia of Bible Truths* for helping me to make the crucial connections between each academic discipline and God's Word.

3. *Home Education and the Clash of Two Worldviews*, Tom Eldredge

4. terms used by C.S. Lewis in *The Lion, the Witch, and the Wardrobe*

5. http://standupforthetruth.com/2016/02/what-do-many-professing-christians-really-believe/ – accessed September 1, 2016

Chapter 5: Why Not Government Schooling?

1. https://www.washingtonpost.com/news/grade-point/wp/2016/04/06/remedial-classes-have-become-a-hidden-cost-of-college/ – accessed September 2, 2016

ENDNOTES, LINKS, & REFERENCES

2. https://www.washingtonpost.com/local/education/us-student-performance-slips-on-national-test/2015/10/27/03c80170-7cb9-11e5-b575-d8dcfedb4ea1_story.html – accessed September 3, 2016

3. https://www.washingtonpost.com/local/education/study-says-standardized-testing-is-overwhelming-nations-public-schools/2015/10/24/8a22092c-79ae-11e5-a958-d889faf561dc_story.html?tid=a_inl – accessed September 3, 2016

4. http://www.npr.org/sections/ed/2015/10/28/452550976/test-scores-are-falling-is-the-sky – accessed September 3, 2016

5. http://freakonomics.com/2011/09/01/were-colonial-americans-more-literate-than-americans-today/ – accessed September 3, 2016

6. http://www.av1611.org/kjv/kjv_easy.html – accessed September 3, 2016

7. http://www.impact-information.com/impactinfo/newsletter/plwork15.htm – accessed September 3, 2016

SLOW SCHOOLING

8. https://search.yahoo.com/yhs/search;_ylt=AwrT6V33UMtXqugAVgcnnIlQ;_ylc=X1MDMTM1MTE5NTY4NwRfcgMyBGZyA3locyltb3ppbGxhLTAwMQRncHJpZAN6OFZaS3VTRVJyT1hwaHlOdWIlT2hBBG5fcnNsdAMwBG5fc3VzZwMxMARvcmlnaW4Dc2VhcmNoLLnlhaG9vLmNvbQRwb3MDMDARwcXNOcgMEcHFzdHJsAzAEcXNOcmwDMzMEcXVlcnkDZnVuZHJhaXNpbmcrMjBzY2hvb2wrMjBhc3NlbWJsaWVzBHRfc3RtcAMxNDcyOTQyMzM3?p=fundraising+school+assemblies&fr2=sb-top&hspart=mozilla&hsimp=yhs-001–accessed September 3, 2016

9. http://www.governing.com/gov-data/education-data/state-education-spending-per-pupil-data.html–accessed September 3, 2016

10. http://www.historyplace.com/worldwar2/hitleryouth/hj-timeline.htm–accessed September 3, 2016

11. https://www.lifesitenews.com/news/ontario-school-board-tells-parents-they-cant-opt-out-of-gay-lessons–accessed September 3, 2016

ENDNOTES, LINKS, & REFERENCES

12. http://www.wnd.com/2016/06/school-sends-deputy-to-warn-7-year-old-about-bible-verses/ – accessed September 3, 2016
13. https://answersingenesis.org/christianity/church/yes-we-are-losing-millennials/ – accessed September 3, 2016
14. http://www.wnd.com/2006/11/38704/ – accessed September 3, 2016

Chapter 6: On Being "Qualified" to Teach

1. https://www.hslda.org/docs/nche/000002/00000214.asp – accessed September 18, 2016

Chapter 9: Toddlers to Big Kids

1. There are some studies that show that preschool is effective for "at risk" students (presumably from broken families, because other studies have shown that neither higher income nor greater parental education equates to better educational results, even in homeschooling), but even there, a key component in what works is, "Parental

SLOW SCHOOLING

involvement is intensive, and integral to the lessons. Parents are taught how to continue their child's learning at home." Also, consider a recent study done by UC Berkeley about how preschool actually *harms* social and emotional development. Another study found that "the more time children had spent in nonmaternal child care across the first 4.5 years of life, the more adults reported conflict with the child and such problem behaviors as aggression, disobedience, and assertiveness." Is it no wonder parents count the days until summer vacation are over? These studies are easy to find, but I do not make the case for keeping children home by study, but by the authority of the Word of God, which states that children are a blessing from the Lord unto their parents, and ought to be diligently raised up in the nurture and admonition of the Lord by those same parents (Psalm 127:3-5, Ephesians 6:4b).

2. Books include: *Shepherding a Child's Heart* by Tedd Tripp, *Let Us Highly Resolve* by Davide

ENDNOTES, LINKS, & REFERENCES

and Shirley Quine, and *Hints on Child Training* by H. Clay Trumbull.
3. *The Three R's* by Ruth Beechick

Chapter 11: Life Skills
1. *Respect the Spindle: Spin Infinite Yarns with One Amazing Tool* by Abby Franquemont
2. https://www.amblesideonline.org/CMAttainments.shtml—accessed 2016
3. http://www.bullittcountyhistory.com/bchistory/schoolexam1912.html—accessed 2016
4. http://www.titus2.com/—accessed 2016
5. http://www.keepersofthefaith.com/—accessed September 3, 2016

Chapter 12: Experiences
1. See https://4-h.org/ for local club listings—accessed January 4, 2017
2. See http://www.wcwa.net/ for local club listings—accessed January 6, 2017

SLOW SCHOOLING

Chapter 14: Teaching Writing

1. *Encyclopedia of Bible Truths: Language Arts/ English* by Ruth C. Haycock
2. https://www.nytimes.com/2014/06/03/science/whats-lost-as-handwriting-fades.html?smid=tw-nytimes&_r=1 —accessed January 20, 2017

Chapter 15: Teaching Reading

1. *Teach Your Child to Read in 100 Easy Lessons* by Siegfried Engelmann, Phyllis Haddox, and Elaine Bruner. (The downside of this book is that I had to write all over it so that the phonics would make sense in spelling).
2. See Beautiful Feet Books, for example https://bfbooks.com/ Also, the Institute for Excellence in Writing incorporates good literature in many of their studies.

Chapter 16: Teaching History, Science, and Math

1. See *Encyclopedia of Bible Truths* by Ruth C. Haycock for valuable resources in

ENDNOTES, LINKS, & REFERENCES

understanding the truth and relevance of the Bible in each school subject.
2. Watch the video series *Untethered* by Wretched Radio to hear the current postmodern thinking infecting college campuses in our day. https://wretched.org.

Chapter 17: Teaching the Fine Arts
1. *Encyclopedia of Bible Truths* by Ruth C. Haycock
2. http://www.traillifeusa.com/
3. https://www.americanheritagegirls.org/
4. Our family has enjoyed https://www.artsattack.com/atelier/index very much throughout the years for excellent art lessons.

Chapter 18: Real Life Helps Along the Way
1. https://www.christianheritageonline.org/product/exposing-a-trojan-horse/ —accessed 2017
2. http://www.flylady.net/ —accessed 2017
3. The first time I was made aware that properly prescribed prescription medications were the 4th

leading cause of death in the US was in 1998 when JAMA published, "Incidence of adverse drug reactions in hospitalized patients." (April 15, 1998). Since then other research has come out that supports it even further.

4. Prevalence in children: Allergies (approx. 1 in 4, 27.2%, 2021); Asthma (approx. 1 in 12: ~16% black, ~7% white, 2016); Autism (1 in 36, 2020). https://cdc.gov – accessed September 4, 2023

5. With thanks to Neil Postman, *Amusing Ourselves to Death*

6. 4.7 hours of TV per day –Bureau of Labor and Statistics. 2015

7. See my blog post: "On Screens and Health." October 27, 2015. https://ahappyhomemedia.com/on-screens-and-health

8. A very helpful book in this regard is *Media Choices* by Philip Telfer.

9. Read my own book, *Present*, for how I struggled to be free from addiction:
https://ahappyhomemedia.com/buypresent

ENDNOTES, LINKS, & REFERENCES

10. Health concerns with Plastic Toys (including BPA plastic): Eco-Healthy Child Care. Children's Environmental Health Network. July 2014. https://health.ucdavis.edu/mindinstitue/resources_pdf/Plastics_and_Plastic_Toys_7_14.pdf
11. Dean Cliver, PhD, University of California at Davis, found that wood cutting boards contained less salmonella bacteria than plastic. With wood, bacteria sank "down beneath the surface of the cutting board, where they didn't multiply and eventually died off." – Journal of Food Protection. 57 (1). 1994.

"Slow School" (The Original Blog Post)

Ideas for Daily Slow School:

- Bible: *Proverbs* video (http://solvefamilyproblems.org); Independent study (Kay Arthur's materials or *Studying God's Word*); Scripture Memory Fellowship
- Read Aloud: lunch time (currently reading *Swiss Family Robinson* and *The Fallacy Detective*)...we will pull out unknown words and assign them for

SLOW SCHOOLING

looking them up in that old-fashioned thing called a "dictionary."

- WOD: (word of the day)...one word, discuss Latin/Greece roots, definition, etc.
- Sketch Challenge (sketchchallenge.blogspot.com)
- Reading
- Math
- Spelling (we use *Spell to Write and Read*)
- Journaling
- Personal study: whatever topic (which is usually science or history related)
- Grammar/handwriting: read aloud passage, copy or dictate, check & rewrite as needed, Webster's dictionary work, diagramming, project or report
- Animal husbandry
- Homemaking chores (why is learning how to do laundry less important than algebra?)

Ideas for Weekly Slow School:

- Research topic...we've been picking topics out of a box, researching and writing reports, and then presenting them to our family. If you ever want

ENDNOTES, LINKS, & REFERENCES

your kids to really learn something, have them try to teach it!
- Handwriting: write out memory verses, make grocery lists, etc.
- Math games
- Knowledge questions ....put up 5 trivia questions, such as "What is REM sleep?" or "How many teaspoons in a tablespoon?"
- Draw a topic out of a hat–talk on it immediately for one minute
- Write a letter
- Play board games...and turn off those screens
- *Handbook of Nature Study* by Anna Botsford Comstock
- Science experiment/lab
- Art/craft

Extras

1. Learn more about our daughters with Down syndrome by listening to the podcast episodes my husband and I recorded.
   —Ruby's story (2013):

SLOW SCHOOLING

https://ahappyhomemedia.com/rubypodcast;

—Poppy's story (2015):

https://ahappyhomemedia.com/poppypodcast

Jottings

SLOW SCHOOLING

JOTTINGS

SLOW SCHOOLING

JOTTINGS

SLOW SCHOOLING

JOTTINGS

SLOW SCHOOLING

JOTTINGS

SLOW SCHOOLING

JOTTINGS

SLOW SCHOOLING

JOTTINGS

SLOW SCHOOLING

JOTTINGS

SLOW SCHOOLING

OTHER BOOKS BY KERI MAE

PRESENT: *How one woman pulled the plug on distraction to connect with Real Life*

AHappyHomeMedia.com/Present

PRACTICES: *Morning and Evening—helping moms have happier homes*

AHappyHomeMedia.com/Practices

FROM MY KITCHEN TABLE: *Mothering in the World... Grounded in the WORD*

AHappyHomeMedia.com/From-My-Kitchen-Table

Available at Amazon.com and other online book sellers.

A Happy Home Media

*Happy is that people, that is in such a case:
yea, happy is that people, whose God is the Lord.*

—Psalm 144:15

Made in the USA
Coppell, TX
10 October 2023